Gary Maclean's Scottish Celebrations

First published in the UK in 2023
by Black & White Publishing Ltd
Nautical House, 104 Commercial Street, Edinburgh, EH6 6NF.

A division of Bonnier Books UK
4th Floor, Victoria House, Bloomsbury Square, London, WC1B 4DA.
Owned by Bonnier Books
Sveavägen 56, Stockholm, Sweden.

Text copyright © Gary Maclean 2023

All food photography by Susie Lowe
All landscape photography by Stewart Ferguson/Cosmic Photography
All illustrations © Yevheniia Lytvynovych/Shutterstock.com
Photo on page viii © SST/Alamy Stock Photos
Photo on page 280 by David Ho & Sandie Knudsen, Headshots Scotland

All rights reserved.
No part of this publication may be reproduced, stored or
transmitted in any form by any means, electronic, mechanical, photocopying
or otherwise, without the prior written permission of the publisher.

The right of Gary Maclean to be identified as Author
of this work has been asserted by him in accordance with the
Copyright, Designs and Patents Act 1988.

The publisher has made every reasonable effort to contact copyright
holders of images and other material used in the book. Any errors are
inadvertent and anyone who for any reason has not been contacted is
invited to write to the publisher so that a full acknowledgement can be
made in subsequent editions of this work.

A CIP catalogue record for this book is available from the British Library.

1 3 5 7 9 10 8 6 4 2

ISBN: 978 1 78530 470 5

Layout by Black & White Publishing
Printed and bound in China

www.blackandwhitepublishing.com

Gary Maclean's Scottish Celebrations

Treasured traditions and contemporary recipes from Scotland

Food photography by Susie Lowe

BLACK & WHITE PUBLISHING

To my beloved wife, Sharon.
Thank you for being my constant source of love and encouragement.

To my children – Cameron, Ewan, Laura, Eilidh, Finlay and Harris –
I dedicate this book to you.
You are the inspiration behind everything I do.

CONTENTS

Foreword by Brian Cox   1
Introduction by Gary Maclean   3
Before You Start   5

NEW YEAR'S DAY

Smoked Salmon with Scrambled Eggs   11
Black Pudding with Kale & Baked Eggs   13
Grilled Kippers with Dulse Seaweed Butter   15
Porridge   17
Pork & Haggis Sausages   19
Chicken Tikka Masala   21
Kale Brose   25
Crispy Potato & Broad Bean Salad   26
Orkney Broonie   29
Chocolate & Coconut Meringues   30

BURNS NIGHT

Address to a Haggis   35
Water Biscuits with Orkney Crab   36
Haggis Croquettes   38
Nowt's Tail   41
Haggis, Neeps & Tatties   42
Brown Bread   45
Whisky & Heather Honey-Cured Sea Trout   47
Clams with Bacon & Kale   48
Cullen Skink Tart   50
Steamed Halibut with Salmon Mouse   53
Whisky & Orange Chocolate Fondant Pudding   55
Cranachan Cheesecake   59

EASTER

Poached Salmon with a Caper Herb Sauce   64
Roast Beetroot with Barley & Clava Brie   66
Pan-Seared Mackerel with Potato, Fennel &
    Herb Salad   68
Roasted Jerusalem Artichoke with Broad
    Beans, Buckwheat & Tomato   71
Shoulder of Lamb Stew   73
Eyemouth Fish Pie   75
Hot Cross Buns   77
Rhubarb Custard & Crumble   81
Rhubarb Crisps   83
Simnel Cake   83
Paisley Almond Cakes   87

SCOTTISH WEDDINGS

Mini Cheese, Onion & Spinach Bridies	92	Twice-Baked Mull Cheddar Soufflé	103
King Scallop with Brown Crab, Barley & Spinach	94	Razor Clams	107
		Crispy Oysters	108
Pan-Seared Langoustine	97	Lamb & Haggis Wellington	111
Pan-Seared Skate Wing	99	Bramble Custard Tarts	113
Confit Duck Leg Salad	101		

HIGHLAND GAMES & FESTIVALS

Langoustine Bisque	121	Hot Smoked Salmon & Crab Fishcakes	131
Corned Beef Brisket Sandwich	122	Slow-Cooked Pork Shoulder Sandwich	135
Lobster & Crab Macaroni	125	Short Rib of Beef Pastries	136
Chippy Pickled Onions	127	Winkles	138
Fish Supper	128	Grilled Lobster	141

THE GLORIOUS TWELFTH

Pan-Seared Loin of Venison	145	Classic Roast Woodcock	158
Pot Roast Pheasant	148	Pan-Seared Fillet of Cod	161
Roast Mallard Confit Leg	151	Scottish Game Pie	162
Roast Partridge	155	Date & Walnut Bread	164
Roast Grouse	156	Raspberry Pudding	167

HALLOWEEN

Baked Butternut Squash	172	Fly Cemetery Cake	183
Apple Frushie	175	Highland Toffee	184
Barley Sugar	177	Plum, Cinnamon & Honey Tarts	187
Candy Apples	178	Jam Roly Poly	189
Cinder Toffee	181	Oatie Scones	191

ST ANDREW'S DAY

Mussel Bree	196	Pan-seared Plaice	207
Grilled Langoustine	198	St Andrew's Veggie Pie	211
Haggis Fritter	200	Spiced Ribeye Steak	213
Grilled King Scallops	202	Mary, Queen of Scots Tartlets	215
Chicken in the Heather	205	Winter Plum, Hazelnut & Chocolate Cake	217

CHRISTMAS

Carnegie Brie & Cranberry Bites	222	Brussels Sprouts	236
Cranberry & Sage Sausage Rolls	224	Goose-Fat Roast Potatoes	237
Panko & Scottish Cheddar Brussels Sprouts	226	Turkey Wellington	238
Parsnip & Smoked Cheddar Soup	229	Christmas Pudding	241
The Best Christmas Turkey	231	Mince Pies	243
Pork, Apple & Sage Stuffing	233	Humbugs	246
Honey Roast Parsnips	234		

HOGMANAY

Tear & Share Bread	252	Fillet of Sole	263
Mini Pancakes with Smoked Salmon & Chive Cream Cheese	255	Snowballs	264
		Cream Cookies	267
Roasted Winter Root Vegetable Soup	256	Shortbread Almond & Apple Bake	269
Short Rib of Beef & Haggis Pie	259	Ecclefechan Tart	271
Seared Monkfish Wrapped in Cured Ham	260		

GLOSSARY, CONVERSIONS & INDICES

Glossary	274
Conversion Charts	275
Recipe Indices	276
Acknowledgements	279
About the Author	280

FOREWORD
by BRIAN COX

There should be cause for celebration in everyone's lives; rich or poor. And when our celebratory gatherings involve food, that too should be for everyone. Throughout Scottish history, food has been at the centre of celebrations for everyone; whether well-off or needy. Growing up, myself, in a less than well-off family in Dundee as the youngest of five, my mother, a spinner, able to work only intermittently after the death of my father when I was eight, I still remember meals that were real celebrations.

Clootie dumplings, Forfar bridies, haggis, mince and tatties were meals for all. Maybe vegetables and fruit if you had your own garden patch. Fish caught yourself because nowhere in Scotland is that far from the river or sea. Raspberries and brambles picked in the wild. Historically even oysters and lobster were considered food for the poor. Everyone in Scotland could enjoy similar celebratory meals no matter what their economic situation. And it is this universality that Gary brings to *Scottish Celebrations*.

Since joining the Dundee Repertory Theatre when I was 14, I've been fortunate to make a career as an actor. For over 60 years now, I've travelled the world for films, TV and the theatre. And in those journeys I've seen the similarities and differences in food around the globe. So, for example, every culture has its Forfar bridie: in Latin America, called empanada, in India, samosa. And, of course, potatoes, humble tatties, are used the world over to eke out a meal from shepherd's pie to latkes. Gary brings us inspiration and influences from around the world, but these are all very much a celebration of Scotland, both the traditional and the modern.

Wherever we are in the world we use family meals as a way to come together to celebrate major events and holidays, whatever those holidays might be in a particular country. Celebration food is a way not just to strengthen family bonds but to keep history and tradition alive. We borrow from elsewhere and we take our celebrations (Hogmanay, St Andrew's Day and, of course, Burns Night) with us.

And for hundreds of years the Scots have travelled far. For those of us who have moved elsewhere in the world, our Scottish history has come with us and is keenly felt wherever we end up. In fact, it means as much, if not more, to us than to Scots still living in Scotland – there's no taking it for granted for us. There are lots of Burns suppers in Scotland but there are HUGE numbers in America. We never lose our Scottishness, so with my years living in London, Los Angeles and New York, my love for my native country is renewed in celebrations and with the food that, simple or rich, goes with them.

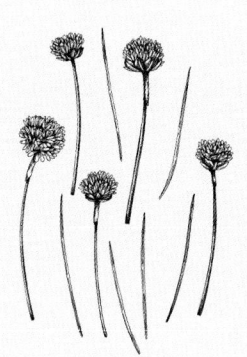

INTRODUCTION
by GARY MACLEAN

As the first-ever National Chef of Scotland, I have spent most of my career promoting Scottish cuisine and culture on a global scale. My passion for food and cooking began at a young age. My family always made the most of the big traditional occasions – like many families we went all-out at Christmas and Hogmanay, and food was at the heart of those celebrations.

It was not until later in my career that I had the chance to see Scotland and Scottish food from a different point of view. My first opportunity to share Scottish food and culture was in the late 1990s when I was asked to head out to Chicago and do a gala fundraising dinner, then perform culinary demonstrations all over the city.

I often think back to that trip and realise that it was when I fell in love with North America – but I have since discovered that it was also the moment I fell in love with Scotland. It gave me the opportunity to see my homeland through someone else's eyes; it allowed me to see how we, as a nation, have impacted the world with our food, heritage and culture. Since then, I have been very lucky and have had the opportunity to travel to every corner of the world to share my love and passion for our amazing food and culture.

Scottish cuisine is a testament to the country's rich and diverse history, and is influenced by numerous cultures and traditions, all of which have shaped it over the centuries. I wanted to write a cookbook that highlights the special celebrations that take place throughout the year and the culinary delights that accompany them.

Each event is steeped in tradition and history, offering a glimpse into Scotland's past and present through the lens of its food and cooking. From New Year's Day to Hogmanay, each chapter provides a comprehensive overview of the event and a tantalising array of recipes that embody its unique character.

Scotland is renowned for its breathtaking scenery, rich history and unique culture. But what many people do not realise is that Scotland also boasts an incredible culinary heritage. With some of the best seafood, world-class meats, and an array of fruit, vegetables and wild game, Scotland's cuisine is a true celebration of its fertile lands and pristine waters.

I hoped to capture the essence of Scottish food and culture by presenting recipes for traditional, modern and timeless dishes, and the festivals that have been an integral part of Scotland for centuries.

The recipes in *Scottish Celebrations* are not just a collection of instructions for making great food, they also tell the story of the country's diverse and unique culinary heritage.

Scottish food is full of family recipes as well, those that have been cherished for generations. Often passed down through generations, with each one adding their own personal touch, recipes become unique to each family, but there are also many classic Scottish dishes that unite us all.

Alongside the traditional recipes, *Scottish Celebrations* features contemporary dishes that reflect the changing nature of our cuisine. But whether old or new, each recipe embodies the spirit of celebration that is at the heart of Scottish culture, from New Year's Day to Hogmanay, and everything in between.

I hope you enjoy the journey and the stories that make Scottish celebrations so unique.

BEFORE YOU START

This cookbook is designed to be fun and user-friendly. One of the most important things to keep in mind while cooking is to stay relaxed! At the end of the day, it's just a plate of food.

With savoury recipes, you have the flexibility to add, subtract or tweak ingredients to your liking. For example, if a recipe calls for 400g (14oz) of mince but your package is 500g (1lb 2oz), feel free to use it all. However, for sweet recipes or ones that involve butter, flour and sugar, it's important to follow the instructions precisely.

When working with **butter**, it's best to choose unsalted.

The **eggs** are always free range.

Two different kinds of **oil** are used throughout the book: good oil and cooking oil. Good oil can be anything from extra virgin olive oil to cold-pressed rapeseed oil, depending on your preference. Cooking oil, on the other hand, is simply meant for cooking and could include sunflower, vegetable or groundnut oil.

All **oven temperatures** in the book are based on fan-assisted ovens. If you don't have a fan oven, increase the temperature by about 10 per cent.

Each recipe in the book is designed to **serve four people** unless otherwise noted.

The primary **measurement** system used is metric, but imperial measurements are included in each recipe, as well as in a conversion chart at the end of the book.

Most recipes can be adapted to be dairy-free and gluten-free; some recipes actually benefit from using gluten-free flour. However, I have yet to find a good egg substitute when baking or dessert-making, but I will continue to test and practise.

GLEN ETIVE

NEW YEAR'S DAY

New Year's Day is a time of renewal and celebration, a chance to start afresh and set new goals for the coming year. Across the globe, people mark this special occasion with a variety of traditions and customs, from fireworks and parades to family gatherings and religious ceremonies. For me, New Year's Day has always been a day of reflection, thinking of the past year and what it meant.

A unique tradition is the Loony Dook. This is a distinctive and modern practice that emerged in the late 1980s. It was born out of the desire of Edinburgh residents to find a remedy for their hangovers. Unwittingly, they initiated a long-lasting custom that has grown over the years. Participants dress up in bizarre costumes and parade through South Queensferry, eventually plunging themselves into the chilly waters of the Firth of Forth.

The day is about having time to relax and recuperate, as we leave the busyness of the festive season and Hogmanay events that are now over. Food tends to be fairly abundant, with plenty of leftovers. In hospitality, it is probably the only day that most places close, so it is a time to properly shut down. There is a real sense of relaxation and peace, and you never feel too guilty that you are doing absolutely nothing.

In this chapter, I have focused on creating recipes that are simple and quick to make, or can be prepared in advance, so that your day of recovery from the night before can be filled with amazing food without you having to make too much effort.

SMOKED SALMON
WITH SCRAMBLED EGGS ON TOAST

Making the perfect scrambled eggs is not as simple as you think, but once you know the rules it is very easy. This is the perfect morning after breakfast or brunch, depending on how late your Hogmanay was. I think there is a touch of luxury in this classic dish – smoked salmon always adds a touch of indulgence. The salmon is traditionally cold smoked over oak wood chips, resulting in a rich taste that pairs perfectly.

I tend to only have this dish around Christmas and New Year. It has become a bit of a ritual at the college where I work, as we always make a point of getting the team together and having a sit-down, and this is the dish we always have.

---

8 eggs

100ml (3½fl oz) double cream

50g (2oz) butter, plus extra for buttering the toast

200g (7oz) smoked salmon

8 slices bread, for toasting, your choice

Salt and cracked black pepper

Small bunch of chives, chopped

Pinch of salad cress, optional

TO NOTE:
Buying high-welfare eggs, such as free-range, makes a huge difference: the extra money spent is worth it.

---

1. Your first task is to whisk together the eggs and half of the double cream. We are going to save the other half for the end. Also, note at this stage we do not want to add any salt – salt will break down the raw eggs and make the cooked eggs watery. We will add salt at the end, as cooked eggs are not affected the same way as raw eggs are.

2. Melt the butter in a non-stick pan over a medium heat.

3. Add the eggs. Cook slowly and gently over a medium heat, stirring with a spatula until soft curds start to form but the eggs are not yet cooked through.

4. Toast your bread.

5. Once the eggs are almost cooked, remove them from the heat and let any residual warmth from the pan finish the job.

6. At this stage you have two choices: shred the salmon and mix it through the hot egg, or keep the slices whole and dress the top of the eggs with it. I have gone with the latter, but if you choose the former, now is the time to mix in the fish.

7. Add the last half of your cream to the scrambled eggs; this will stop them from cooking further.

8. Taste the eggs and adjust the seasoning. I always go heavy on cracked black pepper but easy on the salt, as smoked salmon can be salty.

9. Butter the toast and place it onto serving plates.

10. Divide the eggs between the plates, top with a few slices of smoked salmon (if you didn't add it earlier) and finish with a good sprinkle of chopped chives. Add a pinch of salad cress, if you have some.

BLACK PUDDING
WITH KALE AND BAKED EGGS

This is a hearty start to the New Year! It is super simple, with only a few ingredients – a comforting breakfast that's packed with flavour, bringing together the bold spice of the black pudding with the earthy, vibrant taste of kale and the creamy indulgence of baked eggs. Scotland is renowned for its black pudding and most people will have it in the fridge at this time of year.

400g (14oz) black pudding
100g (3½oz) kale, chopped
2 cloves garlic
Small bunch of flat-leaf parsley, shredded
8 eggs
Small bunch of chives, chopped
25ml (1fl oz) good oil
Salt and pepper

1. Preheat the oven to 190°C (375°F).
2. Cut the black pudding into large dice.
3. Rinse the kale and chop it into small pieces.
4. Heat some oil in a pan on a medium heat.
5. Add the chopped black pudding, cook for 2 to 3 minutes.
6. Meantime, chop the garlic and add it to the pan with the black pudding.
7. Add the chopped kale and cook for 2 to 3 minutes until it is tender.
8. Season with salt and pepper to taste, then mix in the shredded flat-leaf parsley.
9. Divide the mixture between four small baking dishes.
10. Crack two eggs over each portion of kale and black pudding.
11. Bake in the preheated oven for 8 to 10 minutes, or until the eggs are cooked to your liking.
12. Take out of the oven and let the dish cool for a few minutes.
13. Sprinkle with chopped chives and enjoy!

GRILLED KIPPERS
WITH DULSE SEAWEED BUTTER

For those seeking a hearty and flavourful dish to start the year off right, go no further than the classic pairing of kippers and seaweed. It is a delicious choice. The briny saltiness of the smoked fish, sourced from the cold North Sea, contrasts perfectly with the umami richness of seaweed harvested from the rugged Scottish coast.

Gourock lays claim to the first British kippers. According to Colin Milne's *The Story of Gourock*, a gentleman named Walter Gibson, a Glasgow merchant and Provost of the City, made history by curing the first red herring in Britain at Gourock in 1688.

100g (3½oz) butter, room temperature

5g (¼oz) dried dulse seaweed

1 lemon, juiced and zested

1 lemon, cut into wedges

Small bunch of dill

4 kippers

Cooking oil, for the tray

Salt and pepper

1. The first job is to make the seaweed butter. To do this, mix the butter with the dried seaweed, the zest of half a lemon, a squeeze of lemon juice and some chopped dill. Finish with salt and pepper.

2. Take a piece of greaseproof paper and arrange the butter at one end in a sausage shape and roll the butter up in the paper.

3. Twist each end in opposite directions to make a tight cylinder. Pop into the fridge to set. This should take about 1 hour to set hard enough to cut.

4. Preheat your grill to its highest setting.

5. Lay your kippers onto an oiled tray, slice the dulse butter and arrange in the middle of each kipper.

6. Squeeze a little lemon juice on top and place the kippers under the grill.

7. They should only take about 5 minutes to cook.

8. Once they are done, you should be able to remove the bones easily. Serve with a sprig of dill and a wedge of lemon.

PORRIDGE

Porridge for breakfast in Scotland is as iconic a dish as our amazing Cullen Skink or the national dish of haggis. I have never written down the recipe, but feel I have missed out on sharing an incredible recipe with people.

Porridge oats are a perfect start to the day. They contain important nutrients, such as vitamins B1 and B6, as well as zinc, iron and magnesium. Oats are a real superfood – their benefits include lowering blood sugar and cholesterol levels, and, in addition, they are very filling and are very slow-burning, so the body is kept fuller for longer. Oats are among the most nutrient-dense foods you can eat, so porridge should take pride of place in a book that celebrates Scotland's incredible dishes.

I remember the whole salt or sugar debate as a kid, and I am sure in my house it would have been salt. These days I use both: salt for making it, and a little touch of honey to finish. The other great thing about porridge is you can add whatever takes your fancy: apple and raisin compote in the winter, while fresh berries are just as amazing in the summer.

You will always get some chat on how best to stir the porridge: clockwise or anti-clockwise? Predictably, I have found no difference at all. I also think porridge was the first thing I ever cooked on my own. I remember trying to turn leftover porridge into oatcakes by spreading it on a tray and sticking it under the grill. It caught fire almost instantly – a valuable lesson learned for a ten-year-old.

MAKES 4 GOOD PORTIONS

150g (5oz) rolled porridge oats (I also like jumbo oats)
1 litre (1 quart) milk
Pinch of salt
Pinch of ground cinnamon
2 tsp honey

1. Add the milk to a saucepan with the oats and a pinch of salt.

2. Gradually bring to the boil on a medium heat.

3. Once it has come to the boil, reduce the temperature and let it simmer for about 6 to 8 minutes.

4. Make sure you continue to stir, as it can catch very easily.

5. Place into individual bowls and finish how you wish. In the winter, I love a little drizzle of honey and a good pinch of ground cinnamon.

PORK & HAGGIS SAUSAGES

WITH HOMEMADE BAKED BEANS AND TATTIE SCONES

As I am writing this recipe, I can't wait to get away from the computer and get to cooking. Haggis sausages are amazing – the haggis sorts the texture and flavour like nothing else. The addition of homemade tattie scones and beans makes this the perfect start to your new year. You can and should make everything in advance, especially the tattie scones, as they freeze well.

Making your own sausages is really easy; the skins and the sausage gun can be bought online for a few pounds, or you can also use a piping bag.

MAKES 4 TO 6 PORTIONS

For the pork and haggis sausages

Small bunch of flat-leaf parsley, shredded
500g (1lb 2oz) haggis
500g (1lb 2oz) pork sausage meat
1 tsp cracked black pepper
1 metre (3ft) sausage skins (I used 28mm/1in skins)
200g (7oz) cherry tomatoes
Salt and pepper

For the pork and haggis sausages

1. The first task is to shred the flat-leaf parsley. Once done place it in a bowl.

2. Add the haggis and the pork sausage meat. Then add the black pepper and mix well.

3. I use a handheld sausage machine I bought online. Fill the sausage gun with the mixture, then load the skin onto the end nozzle. Tie a knot at one end.

4. Fill the skin, then push out as much of the air as possible and tie a knot at the other end.

5. Twist the filled skins into the length of sausage you need.

6. Cut the sausages off the bunch. You can grill or pan-fry them when needed.

TO NOTE:
The beans need to be soaked overnight and take around 3 hours to cook, but it is worth it.

recipe and ingredients continue on the next page

For the tattie scones

250g (9oz) mashed potatoes
25g (1oz) butter
Pinch of salt
50g (2oz) plain flour

For the homemade baked beans

400g (14oz) dried cannellini beans
2 red onions, finely chopped
2 garlic cloves, finely chopped
1 x 400g (14oz) tin chopped plum tomatoes
25g (1oz) tomato purée
2 tbsp dark brown sugar
3 tbsp malt vinegar
400ml (14fl oz) water
3 tbsp good oil

For the tattie scones

1. A flat iron griddle pan is the best way to make potato scones, though a flat frying pan can also be used.

2. Your first job is to boil the potatoes and then mash them thoroughly. Traditionally families would be using leftover mashed potatoes from the night before.

3. Add the butter and salt.

4. Mix the plain flour with the mashed tatties in a bowl, ensuring the potato scone mixture does not go dry. You might have to add more mash or flour to get the consistency correct. It should be almost like soft pastry.

5. Empty the mixture onto a flat surface and use a rolling pin to roll out the mixture evenly to a height of about 4mm (¼in). Using a 20cm (8in) plate as a guide, cut the mixture into a circle and then cut this into triangles. You could also cut it into smaller rounds; some bakers around the country sell round tattie scones.

6. Put each triangular potato scone into the griddle or frying pan and cook on both sides until brown. Be careful not to have too much oil in the pan.

7. You can make these in advance and reheat, or eat them immediately. You can also freeze them from this stage as well, just make sure you wrap them well before going in the freezer.

For the homemade baked beans

1. Begin by soaking the beans overnight.

2. The next day, drain them and transfer them to a pan.

3. Cover with fresh water and bring to a boil over a medium heat. Let them cook for approximately 45 minutes to 1 hour, or until they're tender.

4. Once done, remove them from the heat and drain them.

5. Using a large saucepan, heat the oil over a medium heat. Add the onions and allow to cook for 6 to 8 minutes.

6. Add the garlic, tinned tomatoes, tomato purée, sugar, vinegar and water, then the beans. Reduce the heat to low and let it simmer for 1½ to 2 hours, stirring occasionally until the sauce thickens and the beans are soft.

To finish

1. Halve the cherry tomatoes and place them on a tray. Drizzle with a little oil and season with salt and pepper.

2. Pop the tomatoes in the oven with the sausages and the potato scones, to reheat.

3. Serve with the beans.

CHICKEN TIKKA MASALA

WITH PILAF RICE

I know what you are thinking: why has a classic Indian curry popped up in a book about Scottish celebrations? First, curry is one of the most popular dishes in Scotland. There is nothing better than a curry to get you back on your feet after a night of celebrating. Second, this curry was invented in Glasgow! Yes, that's right. One of the world's most famous curries is Scottish. The dish was invented by Ali Ahmed Aslam, the chef and owner of the iconic Glasgow restaurant the Shish Mahal. Mr Ali, in response to a customer complaint that the chicken tikka was too dry, added a tin of Campbell's tomato soup into the mix and the legend was born. I have even been able to take this recipe to India and use the sauce as part of a Scottish showcase dinner I was doing at a culinary school.

As a Glaswegian chef, I think this dish deserves to take pride of place in a book dedicated to Scottish food celebrations. I tip my chef's hat to Mr Ali, who was responsible for changing the Glasgow restaurant scene, and for doing so much to enhance the reputation of food in Scotland.

MAKES 4 TO 6 PORTIONS

For the chicken marinade

1kg (2lb 3oz) boneless chicken thighs
2 tsp cumin seeds
2 tsp coriander seeds
250g (8oz) plain yoghurt
3 red chillies
3cm (1in) root ginger, grated
5 cloves garlic
2 tsp garam masala
½ tsp turmeric
1 tsp chilli powder
1 tsp salt
½ tsp cracked black pepper

For the sauce

4 medium onions, finely diced
5 cloves garlic, finely grated
2 red chillies, finely chopped
3cm (1in) root ginger, finely grated
1½ tsp garam masala
1 tsp turmeric powder
1 tsp red chilli powder
1½ tsp cumin seeds
1 tsp coriander seeds
1x 305g (11oz) tin tomato soup
1 tsp sea salt
200ml (7fl oz) double cream
1 tsp mango chutney
Small bunch of coriander, shredded
50ml (2fl oz) cooking oil

For the pilaf rice

1 onion, finely diced
200g (1 cup) long grain rice
300ml (1¼ cups) stock, 1 stock cube
1 bay leaf
25ml (1fl oz) cooking oil
50g (2oz) butter

recipe continues on the next page

For the chicken

1. Your first task is to marinate the chicken thighs. Before doing that, trim the thighs and remove the skin. I love chicken skin, but for this recipe, for the marinade to work, it is better removed. Also, make sure you have taken out the bones and any little pieces of cartilage.

2. Next, in a dry frying pan, dry roast the cumin seeds and coriander (to toast the spices from the sauce portion of the recipe at the same time). Once the seeds start to pop and crackle, they are ready to be ground. You can do this in a pestle and mortar or a spice blender. You could substitute the whole spice with pre-ground, but doing it fresh makes an incredible difference.

3. In a blender (using the ingredients from the marinade list only) add the yoghurt, red chillies, freshly grated ginger, garlic, garam masala, turmeric, chilli powder, salt, cracked black pepper and about half of your freshly ground coriander and cumin seeds. Blitz until smooth.

4. Take a large bowl or a large food bag and mix the chicken with the marinade, making sure you get the marinade into all the nooks and crannies of the chicken. Let it marinate for a minimum of two hours, or overnight if time allows.

5. Once the chicken has marinated, heat the oil in a large frying pan over a medium-high heat.

6. When sizzling, add the chicken pieces in two or three batches, making sure not to crowd the pan.

7. Fry until the chicken is browned on each side. Set aside. This stage is only to brown the chicken; it will finish cooking in the sauce.

For the sauce

1. In a large pan, fry the onions until soft, add the garlic, chopped chillies and ginger, and cook for 2 to 3 minutes. Then add the garam masala, turmeric, red chilli powder, and your remaining ground cumin and coriander seeds. Fry for about 1 minute. Keep stirring at this stage, as the dry spices can burn easily.

2. Pour in the tomato soup and add the salt. Let it all simmer for about 10 to 15 minutes, stirring occasionally until the sauce thickens.

3. Stir the double cream and the mango chutney.

4. Add the browned chicken and its juices back into the pan and cook for an additional 20 minutes until the chicken has cooked through and the sauce is thick and bubbling.

5. Stir in the coriander and top with sliced red chilli. Serve with pilaf rice.

For the pilaf rice

1. Use a pan with a tight-fitting lid. Heat the oil in the pan, then add the onion and sweat for 4 to 5 minutes without colouring.

2. Add the rice and toast it for 1 minute, coating the rice in the butter. Now add the stock and the bay leaf. Bring it to the boil and put the lid on.

3. Place in a preheated oven at 170°C (340°F) for 18 minutes or until the rice has absorbed all the stock. Allow the rice to stand once out of the oven and fluff it up with a fork.

KALE BROSE

A brose is a broth that is thicker than a porridge and more sustaining; this is Scottish cooking at its simplest and finest. Its (very few) ingredients will be sure to fill you with warmth and nutrition. I have seen some recipes that use a big ham knuckle, and I am sure, historically, whatever you happened to have would have been included. I have added one non-traditional ingredient to the soup – a small amount of double cream, just to help bring it together.

MAKES 4 TO 6 PORTIONS

1½ litres (1½ quarts) chicken or vegetable stock
250g (9oz) porridge oats
500g (1lb 2oz) curly kale
100ml (3½fl oz) double cream
Salt and pepper

1. A good quality stock is best for this. Something made from a roast chicken would bring out the very best in this dish. Bring your chosen stock to the boil.

2. Once the stock is boiling, reduce the heat and add the porridge oats.

3. Let it cook for 10 to 15 minutes, making sure you give it a stir every now and then.

4. Meanwhile, wash the kale and tear the soft leaves from the hard stems, discarding the stems.

5. Shred the kale as finely as you can.

6. Add the kale into the boiling mixture and cook for 8 to 10 minutes until tender.

7. Remove from the heat and stir in the double cream. Check the seasoning. You might need to add a little more stock, if you would like it to be more like a soup.

CRISPY POTATO & BROAD BEAN SALAD
WITH PICKLED ONIONS AND TOMATO MAYONNAISE

This is a brilliant, quick and easy dish. The stars of the recipe are the wonderful potatoes – the addition of semolina makes them super-crispy and transforms them into something extraordinary. What many people don't know is that Scotland is one of the largest producers of seed potatoes, which are exported all over the world. So the next time you travel and are tucking in, you might be eating Scottish potatoes.

This recipe ended up being a centrepiece at a Scottish dinner I did in Delhi. I had written a wonderful menu – full of Scottish fish and shellfish – until I realised that 75 per cent of the room had opted for the vegetarian menu. It went down very well and I learned a valuable lesson: the next time I am asked to showcase Scottish cuisine in India, I am going with 100 per cent plant-based recipes.

500g (1lb 2oz) baby potatoes
250g (9oz) broad beans (frozen or fresh)
2 small red onions, sliced
Bunch of flat-leaf parsley, shredded
Few sprigs of mint, shredded
100g (3½oz) chippy pickled onions, sliced
100g (3½oz) mayonnaise
25g (1oz) ketchup
A few drops of Tabasco sauce
2 cloves garlic, minced
50g (2oz) semolina
100g (3½oz) mixed leaves
100g (3½oz) cherry tomatoes, halved
2 tbsp good oil
Salt and pepper, to taste

TO NOTE:
You can vary the ingredients for this dish – most likely, you will need to make it with what is left over in the fridge, but most things will go well with the amazing potatoes.

---

1. Wash the baby potatoes and put them in a pot. Cover with water and add a good pinch of salt. Slowly bring to the boil, then turn down to a simmer.

2. While the potatoes are cooking, prepare the broad beans. If you are using them fresh, remove them from their pods and blanch them for about 3 to 5 minutes. Once cooked, rinse them with cold water and set aside. If you are using them frozen, just defrost them and shell them.

3. When the potatoes are tender, drain them and let them cool naturally in the colander. This will help dry them out. Once the potatoes are cool, slice them.

4. Next, slice the red onion and shred the parsley and the mint. Slice the pickled onions.

5. Mix the mayonnaise, ketchup, shredded mint and Tabasco sauce.

6. Pop a large frying pan onto the stove and, once hot, add a drizzle of oil, place the potatoes into the pan and pan-fry. Add the minced garlic and season with salt and pepper and dust with the semolina. The semolina is going to help make the potatoes super crispy.

7. In a large bowl, mix the cooked potatoes with the broad beans, red onion, parsley, tomatoes and pickled onion.

8. Lastly, add the mixed leaves and give the mix a good toss. Give your salad a generous sprinkle of salt and pepper, and serve your tomato mayonnaise on the side.

ORKNEY BROONIE

Broonie comes from the Norse word *bruni*, meaning thick bannock. It is like an oatmeal gingerbread. I first saw it in a very old cookery book from Orkney. It is also found on the Shetland Isles, where it is known as a runnie. A broonie is a bit of an all-rounder. This delightful gingerbread is perfect for pairing with a warm cup of milk tea during a cold and dark Scottish winter evening, or with a scoop of ice cream on a summer's day.

MAKES 10 TO 14 SLICES

170g (6oz) porridge oats
170g (6oz) self-raising flour
Pinch of salt
1 tsp ground ginger
1 tsp mixed spice
85g (3oz) butter, plus extra for buttering the tin
85g (3oz) brown sugar
2 tbsp black treacle
1 egg
300ml (10fl oz) buttermilk

1. Preheat the oven to 160°C (325°F).

2. Combine the porridge oats, flour, salt, ground ginger and mixed spice in a large bowl.

3. In a separate bowl cream the butter and the sugar until the butter is fluffy.

4. In a small saucepan, heat the treacle until it becomes runny.

5. In a separate bowl, beat the egg, then add the warm treacle and mix together.

6. Add the treacle and egg mix to the butter and sugar mix. Next, mix in the buttermilk.

7. Now add the dry mix of ingredients to the wet mix. Combine until everything is mixed together.

8. Pour the mix into a buttered 900g (2lb) loaf tin.

9. Bake for 60 to 70 minutes, then test if it is ready by inserting a metal skewer into the centre. If it comes out clean, it is ready.

10. Allow the cake to cool in the tin for about 40 minutes before attempting to remove it. It is best to cut the broonie the following day, to give it time to set properly.

11. Serve with butter and jam.

CHOCOLATE & COCONUT MERINGUES

This is my variation of Tunnock's Coconut Meringue. My wife Sharon has been talking about these for years. As a kid, she would get a Tunnock's Christmas/New Year box filled with loads of sweet treats and in the box every year there was a Coconut Meringue bar. There were always loads left over that would last well into the new year. Tunnock's bakery, based in Uddingston, has been a Scottish icon since 1890 and makes millions of Tea Cakes and Caramel Logs that are enjoyed worldwide. Unfortunately, I think the Coconut Meringue is no longer made.

MAKES 4 TO 5

4 egg whites (room temperature)
¼ lemon, juiced
200g (7oz) caster sugar
100g (3½oz) chocolate
200ml (7fl oz) double cream, whipped
50g (2oz) icing sugar
¼ tsp vanilla extract
100g (3½oz) desiccated coconut, toasted

1. First, make sure that all of your equipment is spotlessly clean. Any trace of fat can ruin your meringues.

2. Place the egg whites into a large, clean bowl, switch the whisk on to a slow speed and begin whisking for about 3 to 4 minutes.

3. Add a squeeze of lemon juice at this stage. The lemon juice will help strengthen the whites.

4. Increase the speed on the mixer to a medium speed for 1 minute, or until the whites start to take in air and show signs of doubling in volume.

5. Now, whisk at the highest speed and continue whisking through the soft peak stage until stiff peaks are formed. The whites should be cloudy and foamy. You have to make sure the whites are nice and stiff before you add the sugar.

6. Slowly pour the sugar into the mix, while whisking on a fast speed, until you have a stiff and glossy mixture with a satin sheen.

7. Pipe the meringues into 8 to 10 fingers onto a sheet of non-stick parchment paper.

8. To cook the meringues (when I say cook, it's more of a drying-out process), set the oven to 95°C (200°F). This will give you brilliant, white, crispy meringues. The time it takes depends on the size of your meringues and how soft you would like the centre. Mine took about four hours and still had a soft centre.

9. Once the meringues are crisp and cooled, melt the chocolate in a small bowl over a pot of hot water. Drizzle over the crisp meringue fingers.

10. Whip your cream with the icing sugar and vanilla extract until it is stiff, pop it into a piping bag and pipe the cream between two chocolate-covered fingers. Dust the cream with the toasted coconut and enjoy.

MEALT FALLS, ISLE OF SKYE

BURNS NIGHT

As one of the country's most celebrated Scots, Robert Burns has long been immortalised for his romantic poems and social commentary. However, his contributions to Scottish culture go far beyond his literary works. Every year on 25 January, the anniversary of Burns' birth, Scots around the world gather to toast the life and legacy of this beloved bard. Known as Burns Night, this day is a celebration of all things Scottish, with traditional music, dancing and, of course, food. The first Burns supper was held in Ayrshire in 1801, a few years after the poet's death.

The supper has become a long-standing Scottish tradition, a popular event among lovers of poetry and literature, or anyone interested in Scottish culture and heritage.

The evening typically includes a variety of rituals and traditions. One of the most important of these is the presentation of the haggis. It is usually carried in on a silver platter by the chef, held aloft and walked around the room while a piper plays. The host of the supper then recites Burns' famous 'Address to a Haggis' before the dish is ceremonially cut with a knife. I have done this ritual hundreds of times over the years, including a Burns supper at 10 Downing Street, but none have been more memorable than the last one. I was doing a Scottish charity dinner in Chicago and the speaker managed to slice the top of his finger off as he recited the line 'An' legs an' arms, an' heads will sned, Like taps o' thrissle'. What was more impressive was the fact that he didn't skip a beat until the ceremony ended. Unbelievable dedication to ceremony and tradition.

The supper also typically includes toasts to the memory of Burns, as well as toasts to various important people. Often the guests will recite pieces of Burns poetry or sing traditional Scottish songs. The night usually ends with a rendition of Burns' most famous work, 'Auld Lang Syne'.

Over the years, the Burns supper has become a treasured tradition for Scots and their descendants around the world, helping to keep alive the memory of one of our finest poets – the man voted as the Greatest Scot ever. It is a testament to his enduring legacy that the supper continues to be celebrated with such enthusiasm and passion, and its popularity is growing bigger every year.

ADDRESS TO A HAGGIS

Fair fa' your honest, sonsie face,
Great Chieftain o' the Puddin-race!
Aboon them a' ye tak your place,
Painch, tripe, or thairm:
Weel are ye wordy a *grace*
As lang 's my arm.

The groaning trencher there ye fill,
Your hurdies like a distant hill,
Your *pin* wad help to mend a mill
In time o' need,
While thro' your pores the dews distil
Like amber bead.

His knife see Rustic-labour dight,
An' cut ye up wi' ready slight,
Trenching your gushing entrails bright,
Like onie ditch;
And then, O what a glorious sight,
Warm-reekin, rich!

Then, horn for horn, they stretch an' strive:
Deil tak the hindmost, on they drive,
Till a' their weel-swall'd kytes belyve
Are bent like drums;
The auld Guidman, maist like to rive,
Bethankit hums.

Is there that owre his French *ragout*,
Or *olio* that wad staw a sow,
Or *fricassee* wad make her spew
Wi' perfect sconner,
Looks down wi' sneering, scornfu' view
On sic a dinner?

Poor devil! see him owre his trash,
As feckless as a wither'd rash,
His spindle shank a guid whip-lash,
His nieve a nit;
Thro' bluidy flood or field to dash,
O how unfit!

But mark the Rustic, *haggis-fed*,
The trembling earth resounds his tread,
Clap in his walie nieve a blade,
He'll make it whissle;
An' legs an' arms, an' heads will sned,
Like taps o' thrissle.

Ye Pow'rs, wha mak mankind your care,
And dish them out their bill o' fare,
Auld Scotland wants nae skinking ware
That jaups in luggies;
But, if ye wish her gratefu' prayer,
Gie her a *Haggis*!

WATER BISCUITS

WITH ORKNEY CRAB AND A CORAL TUILLE

Water biscuits with Orkney crab and a coral tuille is a deliciously elegant little canapé that is sure to impress any guest. Handmade biscuits make such a difference and are easy to make. They are garnished with a super-thin coral wafer made from squid ink and oil. It's a little luxury canapé that would be suitable for a Burns celebration. I think this dish is a beautiful representation of Scotland's bountiful coastal cuisine.

MAKES 20 TO 25 BISCUITS

For the water biscuits

200g (7oz) plain flour
1 tsp baking powder
50g (2oz) butter, cold, cut into cubes
½ tsp sea salt

For the crab

1 red chilli, finely diced
Small bunch of dill
50g (2oz) mayonnaise
100g (3½oz) Orkney crab meat
Salt and pepper

For the coral tuilles

If you can, I would measure this recipe using the metric measurements.

90ml (3fl oz) water
40ml (1½fl oz) oil, plus extra for cooking
10g (⅓oz) flour
¼ tsp squid ink, or black food colouring

For the water biscuits

1. Preheat your oven to 160°C (325°F) and line a baking sheet with parchment.

2. Place the flour, baking powder, butter and sea salt in a food processor. Whizz for a minute until the butter is completely mixed with the flour.

3. Add 4 tablespoons water and pulse until the dough comes together. If it still feels dry, add a teaspoon more of water and process until you have a soft but not sticky dough.

4. Roll out the dough on a lightly floured surface into a rectangle approximately 50x25cm (20x10in), and as thin as possible.

5. Brush a little water over the surface of the dough, sprinkle a little sea salt on top and lightly press the salt into the pastry. Prick the dough all over with a fork, then cut into 20 to 25 circles with a 4cm (1½in) cutter.

6. Place the biscuits onto the prepared tray – do not worry if they stretch a bit.

7. Bake for 10 to 15 minutes until the biscuits feel dry and sandy but are still pale – they may still feel soft but will harden up when cooling.

8. Transfer to a wire rack and leave until completely cool.

For the crab

1. Chop the chilli and half of the dill (you'll need the rest to garnish the finished dish).

2. Mix the chilli and the herbs with the mayonnaise and the crab meat.

3. Double check the seasoning and put to one side.

For the coral tuilles

1. Blend all the ingredients together.

2. Heat a little oil in a frying pan.

3. Pour some of the mixture into the hot pan. The mix will cook and all the water will evaporate, leaving a super thin coral wafer in the pan.

4. When needed, break the tuille into your required shapes.

To finish

Top each water biscuit with some of the crab and chilli mix. Garnish with the coral tuille and a little sprig of dill.

HAGGIS CROQUETTES

WITH TURNIP SLAW

These crispy and indulgent croquettes are bursting with the rich and savoury flavours of haggis, while the accompanying turnip slaw provides a fresh and tangy contrast. It is a fantastic option if you are hosting a more informal Burns supper, as the dish can be used as a canapé or in a finger buffet. It is not only perfect for any Burns Night celebration but also for any occasion when you want to bring a taste of Scotland to your table with a difference.

MAKES 4 TO 6 PORTIONS

For the croquettes
500g (1lb 2oz) potatoes, peeled and cut into quarters
25g (1oz) butter
300g (11oz) haggis
2 tbsp chives, chopped
100g (3½oz) plain flour
2 eggs
Splash of milk
100g (3½oz) panko breadcrumbs
Salt and pepper

For the turnip slaw
½ medium turnip
1 carrot
½ lemon, jucied
150g (5oz) mayonnaise
50g (2oz) wholegrain mustard
Small bunch of chives, chopped
Salt and pepper

For the croquettes

1. Fill a large pan with cold, salted water. Add the potatoes and slowly bring to a boil. Try not to overcook them, as they will end up waterlogged and make the croquettes difficult to work with.

2. Once the potatoes are cooked, drain them and allow them to steam out for a few minutes. Place them back into the pot and onto the stove. On a low heat, dry them out, then add the butter and the chopped chives, and then mash. You can use a traditional potato masher, but you will get a much better result if you use a potato ricer. You can buy one of these in most supermarkets.

3. Mix equal quantities of haggis and mashed potato together in a bowl.

4. Put the haggis and potato mix into a disposable piping bag and cut off enough of the end so that you can pipe relatively thick cylinders of mix along a clean work surface.

5. Cut a cylinder of haggis and potato into your desired length. It might be helpful at this stage to pop the shaped croquettes in the fridge for 30 minutes to firm up.

6. You are now ready to coat the croquettes in breadcrumbs. You will need three bowls or tubs: one with seasoned flour, another with the eggs and the milk whisked together, and lastly one for the breadcrumbs.

7. To start with, roll the croquettes in the flour, then roll them in the egg and milk mixture, and finally in the breadcrumbs. The theory with this is that the flour will stick to anything, the egg and milk will stick to the flour, and the breadcrumbs will stick to the egg and milk mix.

8. You are now ready to cook. You have a few options: you could deep fry them until golden, you could shallow fry them, making sure you keep them moving, or you could spray them with a little oil and bake them in a hot oven at 180°C (350°F).

For the turnip slaw

1. Peel, then grate your turnip and carrot.

2. Toss them immediately in the juice of half a lemon.

3. Mix with the mayonnaise, wholegrain mustard and chopped chives. Season with salt and ground black pepper.

NOWT'S TAIL

Nowt's tail – or oxtail – soup has been very popular in Scotland for centuries. It was even the starting dish of a recently discovered Burns supper menu from 1927, held by the Tripe Club in Alloa. It appeared alongside some other delightful lost dishes, including Mixty-maxties and Trimlin Tam.

This was my favourite soup when I was a kid. Even though it came from a tin, I just loved it. When I became a chef, I was very keen to learn how to make this classic from scratch. As you can imagine, the difference between homemade and tinned oxtail soup is night and day. Unfortunately, oxtails are not something you can walk into a supermarket and pick up, but you will be able to order them from a good local butcher. The tail is a very hard-working part of the animal; this makes it a tough cut that requires a bit of TLC and time to cook. I can honestly say that this soup is one of the best you can make, and it is worth the effort.

MAKES 6 TO 8 PORTIONS

1kg (1lb 3oz) oxtail
2 medium onions
½ small leek
2 large carrots
4 sticks celery
50 ml (2fl oz) Worcestershire sauce
250ml (8fl oz) red wine
85g (3oz) tomato purée
50g (2oz) plain flour
1½ litres (1½ quarts) beef stock
1 bay leaf
2 sprigs of thyme
1 sprig of rosemary
Small bunch of chives, chopped
25ml (1fl oz) cooking oil
Salt and pepper

1. Preheat the oven to 200°C (400°F).

2. Your first task is to cut the oxtails into smaller joints. Look for the individual joints along the length of the tail and cut between the joints with a large knife. You do not need to hack at it – if you find the joint, your knife will slide through the cartilage with ease.

3. Once you have divided up the joints, season with salt and pepper.

4. Put the oxtail joints onto a roasting tray, drizzle with a little oil and place into your hot oven. Keep them in the oven until you achieve a nice golden colour on all sides. This adds lots of deep flavour to the soup.

5. Next, roughly chop the onions, leek, carrots and celery.

6. Once you have browned the oxtails, remove them from the tray and put them to one side.

7. Place the chopped vegetables into the same roasting tray and cook for 10 to 15 minutes until they become browned and sticky.

8. Next in a large pan, add the roasted vegetables. To that add the Worcestershire sauce and the red wine. Boil this until the volume has reduced by half.

9. Stir in the tomato purée and the flour. Next, add the beef stock and the roasted oxtails.

10. Lastly, add in the bay leaf, thyme and rosemary. Simmer on a low heat for 3 to 4 hours with a lid on, or alternatively place the pot

recipe continues on the next page

into the oven set at 150°C (300°F) for 3 hours until the meat is starting to fall off the bone.

11. When the meat is tender, strain the whole lot through a sieve.

12. You should be left with a rich beef broth; in your sieve, you will find the bones, cooked meat and vegetables.

13. Allow the contents of the sieve to cool, then separate the oxtail meat from the bones. You can discard the bones and vegetables, as they have done their job.

14. You should have a nice tasty bowl of cooked meat. Shred the meat with your fingers, then add it to the broth.

15. Once you are ready to serve the soup, reheat it and double-check the seasoning – you might be able to add more water if the soup is too thick or strong in flavour. Finish with chopped chives.

HAGGIS, NEEPS & TATTIES
WITH ONION CHUTNEY AND BARLEY BROTH

This is a little twist on the ultimate dish for Burns Night celebrations. You simply cannot have a Burns supper without having haggis centre stage. Ever since Burns wrote the 'Address to a Haggis', it has been associated with him. I have done this dish in various forms over the years – I even made a version when I was on *MasterChef: The Professionals*! I have also served it at 10 Downing Street for their Burns Night celebration.

For the red onion chutney
3 red onions, sliced
100ml (3½fl oz) port
1 tsp redcurrant jelly
3 sprigs of thyme, picked and chopped
1 tsp cooking oil

For the haggis
100g (3½oz) haggis
2 sheets Feuille de Brick pastry
1 egg, for wash
Small bunch of microgreens

For the neeps
100g (3½oz) turnip
½ tsp honey
25g (1oz) butter
Salt and pepper

For the broth
1 carrot
¼ leek
1 stick celery
25g (1oz) barley, soaked overnight
250ml (8fl oz) brown chicken stock
25ml (1fl oz) whisky
Small bunch of chives, chopped

For the mashed potatoes
250g (9oz) potatoes
25g (1oz) double cream
15g (½oz) butter
Pinch of salt and pepper
Pinch of nutmeg

recipe continues on the next page

For the red onion chutney

1. The chutney can be made in advance and stored in the fridge until needed.

2. Add the sliced red onion to a little oil and cook down gently for 10 minutes in a medium saucepan.

3. Add the port, redcurrant jelly and chopped thyme.

4. Cook until reduced and you have a sticky onion chutney. Adjust the seasoning and put to one side.

For the haggis

1. Break down the haggis in a bowl.

2. Roll into 15cm (6in) lengths 1cm (⅓in) thick.

3. Lay one sheet of brick pastry onto the table and brush it with egg wash; lay half of the haggis onto the pastry and roll it up tightly. Do the same with the other sheet and the remaining haggis.

For the neeps

1. Peel the turnip and cut into 1cm (⅓in) dice.

2. In a pan, gently cook the diced turnip in the honey and butter until it begins to soften. Once cooked, put it to one side. Season to taste.

For the broth

1. Finely dice the carrot, celery and leek.

2. Cook the soaked barley in boiling water, refresh and drain.

3. Put the stock into a saucepan and bring to the boil. Reduce the brown stock by half – this will intensify the flavour. Add the whisky.

4. Add the cooked barley and heat until it has softened.

5. Next, add the chopped vegetables and heat through.

6. Finally, add the chopped chives.

For the mashed potatoes

1. Boil the potatoes in salted water until cooked.

2. Drain and dry out on the stove.

3. Mash the potatoes with a potato ricer or masher.

4. Warm the cream and the butter in a small saucepan until the butter has melted.

5. Beat the boiled cream and butter into the potatoes. Add the nutmeg and adjust the seasoning.

To finish

1. Place the wrapped haggis into a frying pan with a little oil.

2. Keep the haggis moving in the pan until it is crisp and golden brown.

3. Meanwhile heat the mashed potato, chutney, turnip and broth.

4. Once the haggis is crisp, cut off the ends at an angle and cut the two cylinders in half giving you four portions.

5. Place the hot mash into a piping bag and pipe a spiral of mash onto the plate.

6. Finish with a spoonful of chutney, the diced turnip and the broth. Top with the haggis and microgreens, if you have them.

BROWN BREAD

Making fresh bread at home is much easier than you would think, especially brown bread, as I find that the lift in brown bread is much quicker. Homemade brown bread is also a lot lighter than shop-bought.

MAKES 1 LOAF

For the brown bread

- 300g (11oz) wholemeal bread flour
- 200g (7oz) white bread flour
- 10g (½oz) salt
- 350ml (12fl oz) water, at 37°C (98°F)
- 1 tsp sugar
- 1 x 7g (¼oz) sachet dried yeast
- 1 tbsp oil

1. Sieve both flours, with the salt, into a large bowl.

2. Mix the water, sugar and yeast. The sugar in this recipe will give the yeast a bit of energy and give the bread a better lift.

3. Make a well in the centre of the bowl and add the water mix. Slowly incorporate the flour and water together until you have a rough dough.

4. Tip it out onto the work surface and begin to knead. Use enough flour for kneading until you achieve a smooth dough.

5. Place the dough back in a bowl and cover with cling film. Allow it to prove until it has doubled in size (30 to 40 minutes).

6. Once the dough has proved, knead it again until all the air has been knocked out of it.

7. Gently begin to shape it into the desired size. Place on a floured tray and cover with cling film.

8. Allow to prove for 20 to 30 minutes until it has doubled in size once again.

9. Bake in a preheated oven at 200°C (400°F) for 18 to 22 minutes – time is dependent on the size and shape of loaf made.

WHISKY & HEATHER HONEY-CURED SEA TROUT

WITH CHIVE CRÈME FRAÎCHE AND BROWN BREAD

This is a superb technique for producing an amazing salmon or sea trout dish. We have been curing fish for as long as we have been catching them. The purpose of curing was to extend the shelf life of the fish. Once you have established the technique, you can mess around with flavours and alcohols. I have made this many, many times with both gin and whisky. The combination of the salt and the honey, mixed with the whisky, brings an unmistakably Scottish flavour to the fish. I have used Loch Etive trout in this recipe, but it works just as well with salmon.

MAKES 8 TO 10 PORTIONS

25g (1oz) heather honey

25g (1oz) sea salt

½ orange, juiced and zested

50ml (2fl oz) good whisky

Small bunch of dill, chopped

1kg (2lb 3oz) sea trout, skinned and trimmed

1 tsp fennel seeds, toasted

150ml (5fl oz) crème fraîche

Small bunch of chives, chopped

½ lemon, juiced and zested

1. Combine the honey, salt, orange juice and zest, whisky and half of your chopped dill in a bowl.

2. Take a roll of cling film and lay two or three large sheets over a tray, big enough for the trout. Place half of the salt, honey and whisky mix onto the cling film, then place the trout onto the mix. Add the remaining mix on top.

3. Cover with the cling film until you get a tight trout parcel and place into the fridge to cure overnight.

4. Meanwhile, toast your fennel seeds in a dry frying pan on a medium heat until the seeds start to pop. Remove them from the pan and put them to one side for later.

5. Once the trout has been curing for at least 10 hours, remove it from the cling film and wash it under cold water. Pat it dry with a kitchen towel.

6. Coat the fish with your remaining chopped dill and the toasted fennel seeds.

7. Mix your crème fraîche with the chopped chives, and the lemon zest and juice.

8. When needed, cut your trout into thin slices and serve with the crème fraîche and the brown bread (recipe on the previous page).

CLAMS

WITH BACON AND KALE

I have always loved clams. They are so easy to cook and are fun to eat. This recipe combines crisp bacon and kale, which I think work brilliantly with the sweet clams.

2kg (4½lb) clams, fresh
150g (5oz) bacon, chopped
2 shallots, finely sliced
50g (2oz) butter
200ml (7fl oz) white wine
200g (7oz) kale, shredded
100ml (3½fl oz) double cream
Salt and pepper, to taste

1. Your first job is to clean the clams. Wash them under cold running water and drain them a few times. Sometimes clams can gather sand inside, so rinsing and draining them helps.

2. Discard any clams that are open.

3. Heat a large pot on the stove. Add the bacon and the shallots.

4. Cook until the bacon has started to crisp up.

5. Next, add the clams, butter and the white wine and place the lid on top. The idea is that the heat from the pot creates instant steam, cooking the clams very quickly.

6. Once the clams have opened, add the shredded kale and the double cream, and season to taste.

7. Bring back up to a boil and serve as soon as the kale has wilted.

CULLEN SKINK TART

Cullen skink soup is a real Scottish classic. It is probably one of the best known and loved of all the traditional dishes; the combination of smoked fish, potato, onion and milk is a real winner. These ingredients can be used in loads of different ways, and they work great as a tart. The addition of cheese adds a touch of body to it. I always try and make some sort of Cullen skink variation when I am hosting events around the world. Most recently I made it at the Alaska Highland Games, but instead of using haddock I managed to get some Alaskan smoked halibut.

MAKES 6 TO 8 PORTIONS

For the pastry
200g (7oz) plain flour
100g (3½oz) butter
50g (2oz) Cheddar cheese, finely grated
1 egg
Pinch of salt

For the filling
200g (7oz) potatoes
2 fillets smoked haddock
1 medium onion, chopped
150ml (5fl oz) milk
100ml (3½fl oz) double cream
2 eggs
Small bunch of dill
Small bunch of chives
50g (2oz) smoked Cheddar cheese, grated
Salt and pepper

1. The first task is to make the pastry. Rub the flour, salt and the butter together until you get a sandy texture.

2. Next, mix in the finely grated Cheddar cheese.

3. Add the egg and bring it together carefully without overworking it.

4. Roll it into a ball and push it into a flat disk, then wrap in cling film and chill in the refrigerator for 30 minutes.

5. Once your pastry has chilled, roll it out thinly and place into a 28cm (11in) tin with a removable base.

6. Line the pastry with greaseproof paper and baking beans. Chill again for 10 minutes.

7. Meanwhile preheat your oven to 180°C (350°F).

8. Once the pastry has been chilled, place it into the oven and cook with the greaseproof paper and baking beans until it is crisp, for at least one hour.

9. Meanwhile, dice the potatoes.

10. To prepare the haddock, you have to remove the centre spine. There are also little bones around the edges of the fillets that need to be removed.

11. In a saucepan, cook the onion on a medium heat for a few minutes without colouring, until soft.

12. Next, add the diced potatoes and the milk. Simmer until the potatoes start to soften.

13. Once the potatoes are soft, add the smoked haddock and simmer for a couple of minutes.

14. Strain the milk from the mixture and allow it to cool.

15. Once the milk is cool, whisk in the cream and the eggs, chopped dill, chives, and salt and pepper.

16. Next, add the potato, onion and haddock mixture to the pastry case.

17. Pour the egg, cream and flavoured milk mix into the case. I tend to have the tart in the oven at this point before adding the liquid, as it helps you get loads of filling into the tart without the danger of spilling it.

18. Top with the grated cheese.

19. Bake in the oven for 30 minutes or until the tart has set.

20. Allow it to come to room temperature before cutting.

STEAMED HALIBUT

WITH SALMON MOUSSE, FENNEL, ASPARAGUS, SAMPHIRE AND CAPER BUTTER SAUCE

Halibut is a wonderful fish, not only to eat but also to work with. I have been lucky over the last fifteen years to have been able to use farmed halibut from the island of Gigha. The Gigha halibut system is unique: they use a land-based system of aquaculture, where the fish are grown in large tanks on the shore in fresh seawater. It suits the halibut perfectly. It is an environmentally sound way to produce food; in fact, the water the fish are grown in goes back into the sea cleaner than when it came out.

In the wild, halibut can grow to enormous sizes and at least once a year you will see one pop up in the press, with a chef posing beside it. If you are struggling to find halibut, most other firm white-fleshed fish work just as well.

300g (11oz) salmon
1 egg white
150ml (5fl oz) double cream
Few sprigs of dill, chopped
4x 200g (7oz) halibut portions (other white fish works well too)
100g (3½oz) samphire
Small bunch of asparagus
1 bulb fennel
50g (2oz) butter
1 lemon, juiced
50g (2oz) capers
Few sprigs of salad cress
Salt and pepper

1. Your first task is to make the salmon mousse. For this, you need to make sure that all your ingredients are very cold. Blitz the salmon in the food processor until puréed – make sure you don't blitz it too long, as it can heat up and cook in the food processor. Next, add the egg white and blitz again until mixed in.

2. Place in the fridge for 30 minutes until the mix is cold again.

3. Once the mix is cold, fold in the cream and the chopped dill, season with salt and pepper, and pop the mix into a piping bag. Put it back in the fridge until needed.

4. To prepare the halibut fillets, place them flat on a chopping board and, using a sharp knife on the widest side of the fillet, cut a slice through the fish horizontally until you get to about 1cm (⅓in) from the end of the fillet – making sure you don't cut all the way through.

5. Once cut, open the fillets up and season with salt and pepper.

6. Next, pipe a thick stream of the mousse into the centre of each fillet.

7. Lay out a few sheets of cling film on top of each other on your work surface. Roll your first halibut fillet up so that the salmon mousse is in the

recipe continues on the next page

middle of the fish. Place the rolled-up fillet on to the cling film. Roll the fillet up in the cling film until you have a tight cylinder.

8. Tie the ends of the cling film so that everything stays together. Repeat for the other three fillets and place into the fridge until needed.

9. Next, prepare your vegetables. Pick through the samphire to remove any tough or woody bits and trim off the woody bottom end of the asparagus.

10. Blanch the asparagus and the samphire in boiling water for about 60 seconds. You will notice that both vegetables will turn bright green and, as soon as that happens, remove them from the heat, drain and immediately cool in ice-cold water.

11. Once cooled, drain and put to one side until needed.

12. Shred the fennel as thinly as you can.

13. Your next task is to steam the fish. You will need to steam them for between 20 to 30 minutes, depending on how thick your rolls are. You could also poach them in a pan of water but make sure your cling film is very tight and secure – it might be worth wrapping them in a couple of extra layers.

14. Meanwhile, in a frying pan, slowly cook the fennel in half of the butter. Once it starts to soften, squeeze a little lemon juice into the pan and season with salt and pepper.

15. Remove from the pan. Add the remaining butter to the pan, along with the samphire, asparagus and capers. Cook until everything is hot and season with salt and pepper.

16. To serve, remove the halibut from the steamer whilst still in the cling film and, using a serrated knife, cut each fillet into three pieces.

17. Spoon the fennel onto the bottom of the plate, top with the samphire, then the sliced fish. Finish with the asparagus and the capers, and drizzle with any remaining butter from the pan.

18. Top with some salad cress to serve.

WHISKY & ORANGE CHOCOLATE FONDANT PUDDING

WITH HONEY & HAZELNUT GRANOLA, CRÈME FRAÎCHE AND VANILLA ICE CREAM

Out of all the puddings, chocolate fondant is the one I think I have made the most and it is the most requested. It's surprisingly easy to make and can be adapted to take on different flavours. It is also a very versatile recipe, as it can be made in advance and frozen (if so, freeze before cooking). Cooking times can vary, depending on the size of your fondant, the temperature of the mix and the oven itself. It is worth testing one before committing them all to the oven at the same time.

MAKES 5 PORTIONS

For the fondant

- 125g (4oz) butter
- 50ml (2fl oz) whisky
- 125g (4oz) dark chocolate (70%)
- 3 eggs
- 125g (4oz) caster sugar
- 25g (1oz) plain flour
- 1 orange, zested
- 100g (3½oz) crème fraîche, to finish

TO NOTE:
You should prepare the granola and ice cream ahead of the fondant.

For the fondant

1. Preheat your oven to 190°C (375°F).

2. Slowly melt the butter with the whisky over a low heat in a pan.

3. Once melted, remove the pan from the heat and add your chocolate to the hot butter. If you break the chocolate up small enough, the residual heat from the butter will completely melt the chocolate.

4. In a separate bowl, whisk the eggs and the sugar together until well combined, then sieve in the flour.

5. Add the melted butter and chocolate to the egg, sugar and flour mix. Stir together until well combined.

6. Add the orange zest.

7. Pour into buttered moulds (you could also use a non-stick bake spray that can be found in good cookshops), preferably a small pudding basin or a parchment-lined ring.

8. Bake for 10 to 12 minutes, making sure the centre is still runny.

recipe and ingredients continue on the next page

For the granola

300g (11oz) rolled oats
100g (3½oz) chopped hazelnuts
85g (3oz) butter, melted
125g (4oz) honey
1 tsp vanilla extract
50g (2oz) coconut flakes (or desiccated)
Small bunch of green herbs, optional

For the vanilla ice cream

You will need an ice-cream machine for this recipe.

5 egg yolks
125g (4oz) caster sugar
450ml (16fl oz) milk
150ml (5fl oz) double cream
1 vanilla pod or a few drops of vanilla extract

For the granola

1. Preheat the oven to 150°C (300°F).

2. In a large bowl, add the oats, hazelnuts, melted butter, honey and vanilla extract, and give it a good mix.

3. Tip the granola mix onto two baking sheets and spread evenly.

4. Bake for 15 minutes, then mix in the coconut and bake for 10 to 15 minutes more.

5. Remove from the tray and scrape onto a separate flat tray to cool. You will find that straight out of the oven the granola will still be soft, but once it cools it will harden up. If kept in an air-tight container, the granola should last a couple of weeks.

For the vanilla ice cream

1. Whisk the egg yolks and the sugar together until almost white.

2. Boil the milk and double cream with the vanilla in a thick-based pot.

3. Whisk the hot milk onto the eggs and sugar mixture and stir well.

4. Return to a clean saucepan and carefully cook until it starts to thicken.

5. Pass through a sieve and then cool to room temperature before adding to your ice-cream machine.

To finish

Take a spoonful of the crème fraîche and smear it onto the plate. Sprinkle the granola on top of the crème fraîche, top with the ice cream. Add your cooked fondant and dust with icing sugar. Finish with green herbs, if you have them.

CRANACHAN CHEESECAKE

Cranachan has to be one of the most famous Scottish puddings. It always features at Scottish celebrations. Sometimes known as the king of desserts, it is especially prominent at military dinners. It's an automatic addition to any officers' mess events I have done. The real genius of this dish is the combination of ingredients: cream, honey, oats and whisky. This fantastic combination could be made into any number of desserts and still be amazing. I have opted to go down the cheesecake route – the main reason is that I can get crowdie cheese into the recipe. Crowdie cheese was originally used to make cranachan before modern tastes replaced it with cream cheese.

MAKES 8 TO 10 PORTIONS

For the base
250g (9oz) Hobnob biscuits
125g (4oz) butter, melted, plus extra for greasing the cake tin
85g (3oz) honey

For the filling
100g (3½oz) rolled oats
50g (2oz) honey
50g (2oz) caster sugar
85ml (3fl oz) whisky
500g (1lb 2oz) crowdie cheese
4 eggs
400g (14oz) raspberries

1. Butter a deep 23cm (9½in) springform cake tin.

2. For the base, put the biscuits into a food processor and blitz until broken down. I like to keep a bit of texture to them.

3. Add in the melted butter and honey and process it again until thoroughly combined. Press this mixture evenly into the base of your prepared tin. Place it into the fridge to set while you make the filling.

4. Preheat the oven to 160°C (325°F).

5. In a small pan over a low heat, toast the oats, honey and one teaspoon of the sugar. Keep the pan moving, until the oats are golden, then add the whisky. Heat until the whisky has cooked out.

6. Tip onto a tray to cool.

7. Next put the crowdie cheese, eggs and the remaining sugar into a bowl and mix until smooth.

8. Stir in the cooled toasted oatmeal and whisky mixture.

9. Stir in half of your raspberries.

10. Pour the mixture over the chilled biscuit base.

11. Pop into the oven and bake for 35 to 40 minutes, or until the cheesecake is set around the edges but is still a bit wobbly in the middle.

12. Turn off the oven and leave the cheesecake inside, with the door open, until it is cool. Doing this allows the cheesecake to cool slowly and will help prevent it from cracking.

13. Carefully unmould the cheesecake onto a board and top it with the remaining raspberries.

14. Cut it into portions and serve.

BALGONE, NORTH BERWICK

EASTER

EASTER

Easter is a joyful time of the year, celebrated by millions of people around the world. This spring celebration marks the resurrection of Jesus Christ, one of the most significant events in the Christian faith. Easter in Scotland has been celebrated since the Christianisation of the country in the sixth century. It is traditionally a time of renewal. Interestingly, we associate Easter with the resurrection of Jesus Christ, but this celebration was predated by pagan festivals of renewal and rebirth for thousands of years before the birth of Christ and the Easter story.

In modern times, many Scots celebrate Easter with a large family meal which often includes lamb, fish or ham. Hot cross buns are also a popular Easter treat in Scotland. In my home, we make a real effort to make it a special day. We have an Easter egg hunt that all the kids in the street take part in. This is a real coming together of friends and neighbours, and marks the beginning of spring in a real collaborative style. We have even had a life-sized Easter bunny turn up to entertain the kids. We decorate eggs and roll them down a hill.

Overall, Easter is an important holiday in Scotland and is celebrated with both religious and cultural traditions.

POACHED SALMON

WITH A CAPER HERB SAUCE

Salmon is such a versatile fish. It can be used in a vast number of ways. I might be biased, but I think there is nothing better than Scottish salmon. We have the perfect habitat for raising salmon in Scotland. Interestingly, salmon is the UK's biggest food export – we send Scottish salmon to more than 150 countries throughout the world. One of the best farmed salmon, in my opinion, is called Native Hebridean. It is the only Scottish salmon bred using eggs from Hebridean fish and grown in the Hebrides. The end result is a fish that has wonderful firm flesh and a beautiful flavour.

MAKES 8 TO 10 PORTIONS

For the poached salmon

Small bunch of chives, chopped
Small bunch of dill, chopped
Small bunch of flat-leaf parsley, chopped
½ side Scottish salmon
25ml (1fl oz) whisky
1 tsp curry powder
1 tsp ground cumin
4x 11cm (4in) leaf gelatine sheets
Salt and pepper
50g (2oz) capers, to finish

For the herb sauce

2 or 3 cloves garlic
2 shallots
Bunch of flat-leaf parsley
Bunch of mint
Bunch of basil
4 tbsp capers
1 tsp Dijon mustard
1 lemon, zested
85ml (3fl oz) good oil
Salt and pepper

For the poached salmon

1. The first task is to finely chop all the herbs.

2. Next, take your salmon and cut it into four long strips.

3. Put the salmon strips into a bowl and add the herbs, whisky, curry powder, cumin, salt and pepper. Mix this together to coat the salmon with the herbs.

4. Using a pair of scissors, cut the gelatine sheets in half lengthwise.

5. Take two coated salmon strips and place the cut gelatine between them.

6. Lay out three large sheets of cling film on top of one another.

7. Place the two strips of salmon with the gelatine sandwiched between them at one end.

8. As tightly as possible, roll the salmon up in the cling film.

9. Once wrapped, tie both ends. Repeat for the other two strips.

10. Steam or slowly poach the parcel for about 20 to 25 minutes, until the salmon is cooked.

11. Once cooked and cooled, you can slice it. I tend to keep it in the cling film, as it makes it easier to slice. Once sliced, remove the cling film.

For the herb sauce

1. This is a very easy recipe to pull together. The first job is to finely chop the garlic and the shallots.

2. Next, wash and dry all the herbs, then chop them finely and cut the capers in half.

3. You are now ready to bring it together. In a bowl, add the mustard,

lemon zest and all of your chopped ingredients. Mix, gradually adding the oil until it becomes a paste.

4. Taste and adjust the seasoning.

To finish

Arrange the salmon slices on a plate, with a spoonful of herb sauce and garnish with a sprinkle of capers.

ROAST BEETROOT
WITH BARLEY AND CLAVA BRIE

This dish combines earthy roasted beetroot with nutty barley and creamy Clava Brie cheese. It's a fantastic combination. With its vibrant colours and incredible flavours, this dish is sure to be a hit at any family meal. It is cooked in a risotto style, using barley as a base. Barley is a vital crop for Scotland and Scottish farmers; there is a farm at the end of my road and they often grow barley in the fields. It's fascinating to watch it grow, but even more fascinating to see where it goes once harvested – most of it ends up being made into whisky and shipped all over the world.

400g (14oz) beetroot

150g (5oz) asparagus, blanched and refreshed

2 shallots, chopped

4 cloves garlic

200g (7oz) barley

500ml (2 cups) vegetable stock (a good quality cube would work for this)

100g (3½oz) cream cheese

200g (7oz) Clava Brie (other soft cheese will also work)

25g (1oz) pea shoots, to garnish

25ml (1fl oz) good oil

Salt and pepper

1. Preheat the oven to 200°C (400°F).

2. Peel the beetroot and cut half of it into wedges. Toss the wedges in oil and season with salt and pepper.

3. Roast in the oven for 20 minutes, or until tender and slightly caramelised. Set to one side.

4. Meanwhile, blanch and refresh your asparagus, finely dice the other half of the beetroot. Chop the shallots and garlic.

5. Add a drizzle of oil in a large saucepan over a medium heat and add the beetroot, shallots and garlic. Cook for 5 to 10 minutes, or until softened.

6. Add the barley to the same saucepan and stir to coat it in the oil. Pour in enough hot vegetable stock to cover the barley by about 3cm (1in). Bring to a boil, then reduce the heat and simmer for about 20 to 25 minutes, or until the barley is cooked through and most of the liquid has been absorbed.

7. You should have a wonderfully pink mixture. Add more stock, if necessary.

8. Add the cream cheese and mix together.

9. Cut the Clava Brie into small cubes and add them to the barley mix, stirring until melted and creamy. Season with salt and pepper to taste.

10. Serve in bowls, topped with the roasted beetroot, asparagus and a sprinkle of pea shoots.

PAN-SEARED MACKEREL
WITH POTATO, FENNEL & HERB SALAD

Mackerel is the tastiest fish that comes out of the sea. For some reason, I feel people have forgotten about it. I am not sure why, as it is a stunning fish and very abundant in Scottish waters. Most of the mackerel that is landed in Scotland ends up exported.

It's a very versatile fish and can be used in loads of different ways. While it is wonderful smoked, in this recipe I have opted to grill it. It takes a matter of minutes to cook.

For the salad
4 fillets mackerel
600g (1lb 5oz) baby new potatoes
Small bunch of flat-leaf parsley, shredded
Few sprigs of thyme, shredded
Few sprigs of tarragon, shredded
Small bunch of dill, shredded
1 bulb fennel, thinly sliced
50g (2oz) radishes, sliced
4 spring onions, sliced
100g (3½oz) capers
1 red apple, sliced
Salt and cracked black pepper
Cooking oil

For the dressing
100ml (3½fl oz) good oil
50ml (2fl oz) white wine vinegar
25g (1oz) Dijon mustard
½ tsp sugar
Salt and ground black pepper

1. Your first job is to prepare the mackerel fillets. Place one of the fillets on a board and carefully cut a 'V' down the centre, either side of what is left of the spine bone. If you are careful, you can cut this without cutting the skin, then remove the bones. Repeat with the other fillets.

2. Rub with the oil and season with plenty of cracked black pepper and put to one side.

3. Place the baby potatoes in a saucepan, cover with water and add a good pinch of salt.

4. Bring to a boil and then reduce the heat and simmer until the potatoes are cooked.

5. Once cooked, drain completely in a colander and allow to steam out.

6. Meanwhile, prepare the rest of your ingredients: shred all your herbs, slice the fennel bulb into very thin strips, slice the radishes and the spring onions.

7. Next, slice the potatoes and put them to one side.

8. For the dressing, whisk together all the ingredients, add salt and pepper to taste and put to one side.

9. Gently toss the sliced potatoes with the herbs, radishes, fennel, spring onions, capers and the sliced apple.

10. To cook the mackerel, place the fish onto an oiled tray and pop it under the grill for about 3 minutes. Once cooked, season with a little salt and serve with the potato and herb salad.

ROASTED JERUSALEM ARTICHOKE
WITH BROAD BEANS, BUCKWHEAT AND TOMATO

This recipe could very well be the healthiest I have ever written. It is also full of ingredients that I think people don't use often enough. This dish was inspired by my youngest son, Harris. He is obsessed with growing things, and he had a great crop of broad beans, peas and tomatoes last year. He put a greenhouse on his Santa list and has not looked back since. Not bad for a nine-year-old!

200g (7oz) Jerusalem artichokes
1 tbsp cooking oil
100g (3½oz) broad beans, shelled
100g (3½oz) peas (you can use frozen for this)
50g (2oz) buckwheat, cooked
100g (3½oz) cherry vine tomatoes, quartered
50g (2oz) rocket
25g (1oz) pea shoots
15g (½oz) fresh coriander
50ml (2fl oz) good oil
1 tbsp cider vinegar
Pinch of onion seeds
Salt and pepper

1. Preheat the oven to 200°C (400°F).

2. Place the Jerusalem artichokes in a roasting tin, drizzle with the oil, sprinkle with a pinch of salt and place in the oven for 25 to 30 minutes or until golden and tender.

3. In a separate pan, blanch the broad beans and peas in boiling water for 1 to 2 minutes. Cool, drain and put to one side.

4. While the Jerusalem artichokes are roasting, cook the buckwheat according to the packet instructions. Once done, allow to cool slightly.

5. In a large mixing bowl, combine the roasted Jerusalem artichokes, broad beans, peas, cherry vine tomatoes, rocket, pea shoots and fresh coriander. Mix well.

6. In a small bowl, whisk together the remaining oil, cider vinegar, onion seeds and a pinch of salt and pepper to make a dressing.

7. Drizzle the dressing over the salad and toss gently to coat.

SHOULDER OF LAMB STEW
WITH ROOT VEGETABLES AND GREEN LENTILS

I just love this type of food, using the tougher cuts of meat with loads more flavour. The fact that it's a complete meal in one pot is perfect. Lamb stew is a classic that warms the soul, especially on lazy Sundays. This hearty dish combines lamb shoulder, earthy root vegetables and wholesome lentils, making it a delicious and nutritious meal for any occasion. With its rich and savoury flavour, this recipe is a true taste of home, highlighting the country's love for hearty meals and robust flavours.

800g (1¾lb) diced lamb shoulder

2 carrots, peeled and chopped

2 sticks celery, peeled and chopped

100g (3½oz) baby onions, peeled

½ head celeriac, peeled and chopped

½ bulb garlic, chopped

25g (1oz) tomato purée

25g (1oz) plain flour

175ml (6fl oz) white wine

1 litre (1 quart) lamb stock

2 sprigs of rosemary

2 sprigs of thyme

½ savoy cabbage, shredded

200g (7oz) green lentils, pre-soaked and cooked

Cooking oil

1. Preheat your oven to 150°C (300°F).

2. In a large casserole dish, brown the lamb in a little oil, then remove it from the pan and set it aside.

3. Add the carrots, celery, baby onions and celeriac to the pan on a low heat. Once softened, add the garlic and cook for a further 2 minutes.

4. Add into the pan the tomato purée and flour to create a sticky mix.

5. Add the white wine and reduce it down so that the wine incorporates into the vegetables.

6. Add the lamb stock and the herbs.

7. Pop the browned lamb back into the casserole dish, cover it and put it in the oven for about 2½ hours.

8. Once the lamb is tender, remove it from the oven and then add the shredded savoy cabbage and the cooked lentils.

9. Place back onto the stove, bring to a boil, then check the seasoning and enjoy.

EYEMOUTH FISH PIE

When I think of Eyemouth, I think of fish and shellfish. Eyemouth, in Berwickshire, is a vital port for Scotland's incredible fishing industry. After whisky, seafood is Scotland's second-largest export, sold to more than a hundred countries. I have a selection of fish and shellfish in this recipe, but it is entirely up to you what you use. Your fishmonger will be able to provide you with some great options. My favourite thing about this dish is that it is a complete meal in one – it has everything, and all you have to do once you have prepped is pop it in the oven. Once ready, it can be placed in the middle of the table and everyone can help themselves.

For the mashed potato topping

1kg (2lb 3oz) Maris Piper potatoes, peeled and halved
25g (1oz) butter
Splash of milk
1 egg yolk, optional

For the filling

1 small onion
1 bay leaf
2 cloves
500ml (2 cups) milk
50g (2oz) butter
50g (2oz) plain flour
150g (5oz) Cheddar cheese, grated
250g (9oz) smoked haddock, diced and deboned
100g (3½oz) crab meat
100g (3½oz) lobster meat
250g (9oz) salmon, diced
500g (1lb 2oz) mussels, cooked and out of the shell
1 tsp wholegrain mustard
25g (1oz) chives, finely chopped
4 spring onions, finely sliced
100g (3½oz) frozen peas
Salt and pepper

For the mashed potato topping

1. In a pan of water boil the potatoes for 15 minutes, until tender.

2. Drain in a colander and allow them to steam out. This gets a good bit of the water out of the potatoes; all the steam you see is moisture that you don't need. Return the potatoes to a dry pan and put it back on a medium heat. This stage achieves two things: it gets the potatoes back to being nice and hot (having the potatoes piping hot is vital when mashing them), and it also helps get rid of more moisture.

3. After a couple of minutes, you are ready to mash them with the butter and a splash of milk. Season to taste. You could also add an egg yolk, as it will help colour the potato.

For the filling

1. The first job is to make the white sauce. Start by peeling your onion, then using the cloves to pierce the bay leaf onto the onion.

2. Place the studded onion into a small pot and cover it with milk.

3. Slowly bring the milk up to a simmer. As soon as it's simmering, turn off the heat and allow the studded onion to flavour the milk.

4. Melt the butter in another small pan, then add the flour and mix to form a thick paste called a roux.

recipe continues on the next page

5. Cook out for 3 to 4 minutes, then slowly start to add the warm flavoured milk. Stir continuously while milk is added until you achieve a smooth sauce with the consistency of thick double cream. If you add the milk a little at a time, you will avoid making a lumpy sauce.

6. Cook this out for 10 minutes over a very low heat to avoid burning the sauce, stirring every minute or so.

7. Take off the heat and stir in the cheese.

8. Next add your fish and shellfish, mustard, chives, spring onions and peas.

9. Preheat your oven to 200°C (400°F).

10. Spoon the mixture into an ovenproof dish, or dishes if you are serving individual pies.

11. Next, fill a piping bag with a star nozzle with the mashed potatoes.

12. Pipe the potato on top and sprinkle it with any remaining Cheddar cheese. Add salt and pepper to taste.

13. Place into the oven for 25 to 35 minutes, or until the topping is golden and bubbling at the edges.

14. Allow to settle for 10 to 15 minutes before serving.

HOT CROSS BUNS

The history of the hot cross bun is complex and long. People have been making variations of these for thousands of years – they even predate Christianity. The ancient Egyptians used small round bread topped with crosses to celebrate the gods. The cross divided the bread into four equal sections, representing the four seasons. Closer to home, hot cross buns have been synonymous with Easter celebrations for more than 800 years. You start seeing them in shops almost immediately after New Year. They are very popular in Scotland, and they tend to contain a little more spice than others found elsewhere in the UK.

MAKES 16 BUNS

For the buns
300ml (10fl oz) milk, plus 2 tbsp more
50g (2oz) butter
500g (1lb 2oz) bread flour
85g (3oz) caster sugar
½ tsp ground cinnamon
½ tsp mixed spice
¼ tsp salt
1 x 7g (¼oz) sachet dried yeast
1 egg, beaten
150g (5oz) sultanas
100g (3½oz) mixed peel
1 orange, zested

For the cross
100g (3½oz) plain flour, plus extra for dusting
150ml (5fl oz) water (approximate)

For the glaze
100g (3½oz) apricot jam, for the glaze

1. Your first task is to heat up the milk. Once it seems hot enough to melt the butter, remove it from the heat and add the butter to the milk.

2. Leave to cool until it reaches baby-bottle temperature of 37°C (98°F).

3. Put the bread flour, caster sugar, cinnamon, mixed spice, salt and the sachet of yeast into a bowl.

4. Make a well in the centre. Pour in the warm milk and butter mixture, then add the beaten egg.

5. Mix well, then bring everything together with your hands until you have a rough, sticky dough.

6. Tip onto a lightly floured surface and knead the dough. You don't need a specific method, as long as you are turning the dough into itself. Knead until the dough is smooth and elastic and bounces back when you stick a finger into it.

7. Put the dough in a lightly floured bowl, cover it with cling film and leave to rest until it has doubled in size and a finger pressed into it leaves a dent.

8. At this stage, tip in the sultanas, mixed peel and orange zest.

9. Knead the dough, making sure everything is well mixed. Leave to prove until it has doubled in size again, then cover with cling film.

recipe continues on the next page

10. Once it has doubled in size for a second time, divide the dough into 16 even pieces – approximately 100g (3½oz) balls.

11. Roll each ball on a lightly floured work surface. Arrange them on your baking tray lined with parchment, leaving enough space for the dough to expand.

12. Carefully cover, but not too tightly, with some oiled cling film and set aside to prove. You are looking for the buns to double in size.

13. Preheat your oven to 180°C (350°F).

14. Next, create the mixture for the cross. To the plain flour, add about 10 tablespoons of water to make a paste. Add the water one tablespoon at a time, so you add just enough to make the correct consistency.

15. Spoon this into a disposable piping bag and cut a small tip out of the end.

16. Pipe a line along each row of buns, then repeat in the other direction to create crosses.

17. Bake for 15 to 20 minutes until golden brown.

18. Meanwhile, to create the glaze, heat the apricot jam in a small saucepan.

19. As soon as the buns come out of the oven, brush the hot glaze over the top of the buns and leave them to cool on a wire rack.

RHUBARB CUSTARD & CRUMBLE

Rhubarb and custard is something I have fond memories of. We always had rhubarb growing in the garden, and it was a real treat when it was in season. It was mostly eaten raw with a bag of sugar to dip it in. This is my take on the childhood classic – it is a dish that I developed for a student culinary competition many years ago. It is a bit of work, but I think it is worth doing, especially for a special occasion. It looks more complicated than it is. You will need some stainless-steel rings for this, and a juicer would be an advantage.

This dish is made in stages and is layered: starting first with the top layer, this is set in the ring and you build it up from that. Once all layers are set, it is turned upright, removed from the ring and served. You start with a layer of jelly, then cooked rhubarb, then custard, and finish with the crumble.

MAKES 4 TO 6 PUDDINGS

For the rhubarb jelly
2x 11cm (4in) leaf gelatine sheets
50g (2oz) root ginger
300g (11oz) rhubarb
100g (3½oz) sugar
Cooking oil

For the rhubarb filling
275g (10oz) rhubarb
85g (3oz) sugar

For the crumble
100g (3½oz) plain flour
60g (2½oz) butter
60g (2½oz) sugar

For the custard
4x 11cm (4in) leaf gelatine sheets
570ml (2½ cups) double cream
1 vanilla pod or a few drops of vanilla extract
6 egg yolks
85g (3oz) sugar

For the rhubarb jelly

1. Your first job is to prepare your rings. I have used rings that are 7cm (2¾in) in diameter and 3½cm (1½in) tall. All you need to do is cover one side with cling film tightly without wrinkles or holes.

2. Once the rings are sorted, soak the leaves of gelatine in a bowl of ice-cold water.

3. Next, peel the root ginger and pass it through the juicer.

4. Wash the rhubarb and push it through the juicer, too. If you don't have a juicer, you can blitz it in a blender and then sieve the juice through a cloth or a paper coffee filter.

5. Warm the ginger and rhubarb juice in a pan with the sugar.

6. Measure 142ml (4½fl oz) of the warm juice into a jug and add the soaked gelatine.

7. Spray the rings with non-stick bake spray or rub with a little oil.

8. Once the gelatine has melted, pour a ½cm (⅕in) layer of the jelly into the cling-filmed rings and place it into the fridge to set.

recipe continues on the next page

For the rhubarb filling

1. Preheat the oven to 150°C (300°F).

2. Cut the rhubarb into 1cm (⅓in) lengths and place the rhubarb on a tray, cut side up.

3. Sprinkle with the sugar and bake in the oven for 10 to 12 minutes.

4. Allow to cool.

5. Once cool, place the rhubarb on top of the set jelly in each of the four pastry rings, making sure you fill every gap. Place it in the fridge to chill.

For the crumble

1. Preheat the oven to 160°C (325°F).

2. Place all the ingredients into a bowl and rub to a sandy texture.

3. Put the mix onto a tray and place it in the oven. Bake for 15 to 20 minutes.

4. Every now and then, give the crumble a stir.

5. Once cooked, remove the tray from the oven and allow the crumble to crisp up. Put it to one side.

For the custard

1. Soak the gelatine in ice-cold water until soft.

2. In a pot, put the double cream and the split vanilla pods, or extract, onto the boil.

3. Whisk the egg yolks and the sugar together.

4. Once the cream has boiled, add it to the egg mixture and then put the mix into a clean pan and cook out until thick and creamy, making sure not to boil again.

5. Remove the vanilla pods, making sure you scrape the seeds back into the mix, and add the soaked gelatine.

6. Make sure the gelatine has melted, then mix well.

7. Allow the custard to come to room temperature.

To assemble

1. Pour the custard into the rings, on top of the baked rhubarb, leaving a little bit of room to add the crumble mix.

2. Once you have poured the custard in, top it with the crumble. Then with the palm of your hand, push the mix flat on top.

3. Place the puddings into the fridge to set.

4. To finish the dish, place the ring onto the plate, crumble-side down, and warm the ring with your hands – this should free it and allow you to remove the ring.

RHUBARB CRISPS

If you have time, this is a great addition to the rhubarb crumble on the previous page. It will need to dry out overnight.

100g (3½oz) sugar
100g (3½oz) water
1 stick rhubarb

1. Place the sugar and water into a small saucepan and bring to a boil.

2. Remove from the heat.

3. In the meantime, cut the rhubarb into 7cm (2¾in) lengths and, using a vegetable peeler or mandolin, cut thin strips from the rhubarb pieces.

4. Put the rhubarb strips into the warm sugar syrup and let it wilt.

5. Remove the rhubarb from the syrup, let the syrup drip off and lay them flat on a sheet of parchment paper or a silicon mat.

6. Place the strips into the oven at 50°C (120°F) or in a plate-warming drawer to dry out and become crisp.

7. Serve with your dessert.

SIMNEL CAKE

Simnel cake is a rich fruit cake, with a layer of marzipan in the middle and on top. It is perfect for Easter celebrations. Dating back to medieval times, it was once associated with Mothering Sunday. It has eleven balls of marzipan on top, one each for the eleven disciples who didn't betray Jesus.

Simnel cake is similar to black bun, which is usually served at Hogmanay, but it has a brighter and more spring-like finish. This recipe combines the perfect balance of spices, dried fruits and nuts, creating a deliciously moist and fruity cake.

Simnel cake is not the easiest thing to find in a baker's shop these days – I'm not sure why, as it would look great in the window! The recipe is fun to make and will serve as a wonderful centrepiece for your Easter Sunday table.

recipe starts on the next page

MAKES 8 TO 10 PORTIONS

For the cake
170g (6oz) butter, softened, plus extra for greasing
170g (6oz) light-brown sugar
3 eggs, beaten
170g (6oz) self-raising flour
50g (2oz) ground almonds
100g (3½oz) sultanas
100g (3½oz) glacé cherries, quartered
100g (3½oz) dried apricots, chopped
100g (3½oz) hazelnuts, chopped
2 tsp mixed spice
50ml (2fl oz) milk

For the topping
500g (1lb 2oz) golden marzipan
4 tbsp apricot jam
1 egg, beaten

1. Your first task is to weigh and measure all the ingredients.

2. Grease a 20cm (8in) round, deep-sided, loose-bottomed tin. Line the base with parchment paper.

3. Cream the butter and the sugar together. Once it is light and fluffy, add the beaten eggs a little at a time.

4. Combine the flour and the ground almonds in a large bowl and mix well.

5. In a separate bowl, combine the sultanas, cherries, apricots, hazelnuts and mixed spice.

6. Add the flour and the ground almonds mix into the eggs and sugar.

7. Next, add in the fruit and hazelnut mixture with the rest of the ingredients and fold everything together. Lastly, add the milk and mix well.

8. Spoon half of the mix (550g/1lb 3oz) into the prepared tin and make sure to level the surface.

9. Roll out one-third of the marzipan to the size of the base of the tin and place it onto the cake mixture.

10. Preheat your oven to 140°C (275°F).

11. Scoop the remaining batter on top of the marzipan and again level the surface.

12. Bake the cake for 1 hour 15 minutes to 1 hour 30 minutes. Test if it is cooked by inserting a metal skewer into the cake and if it comes out clean it is cooked. (Test every 15 minutes after the first hour.)

13. Once cooked, allow the cake to cool for 10 minutes before removing it from the tin.

14. Once the cake is cool, heat the apricot jam in a pan and brush it on top of the cake.

15. Roll out half of the remaining marzipan and place it on top of the cake, using your thumb to crimp around the edges.

16. Form 11 small balls with the marzipan that is left and place them around the edge of the cake, fixing them to the marzipan with a little beaten egg.

17. Brush the marzipan with the egg and glaze it under a hot grill, turning the cake to ensure even browning. You can also use a blow torch, if you have one.

18. Allow to cool before cutting.

PAISLEY ALMOND CAKES

These cakes are very easy to make and have the added bonus of being gluten-free. They can be made from start to finish in about 30 minutes. This is a recipe I have been working on for a few years and have used it as a small petit four at posh dinner parties. The history of this little cake is difficult to find, but my reckoning is that its connection to Paisley is the almonds. One of the things the town is best known for is the paisley pattern, which is crammed full of almond-like shapes. I think the cake came after that design.

MAKES 12 CAKES

85g (3oz) caster sugar
85g (3oz) butter, softened, plus extra for greasing the muffin tin
2 eggs
125g (4oz) cornflour
125g (4oz) rice flour
1 tsp baking powder
85g (3oz) ground almonds
50ml (2fl oz) milk
50g (2oz) sliced almonds

1. In a small bowl, beat together the sugar and butter until they are light and fluffy.

2. Beat the eggs and add to the sugar and the butter a bit at a time.

3. In a separate bowl, sieve together the cornflour, rice flour and baking powder.

4. Gradually fold this into the sugar and egg mixture.

5. Next, fold in the ground almonds. Add the milk a little at a time until the mix falls off the spoon.

6. Preheat your oven to 180°C (350°F).

7. Lightly grease a 12-cup muffin tin.

8. Spoon the mixture into the tin, filling each well up to three-quarters full and top each with the sliced almonds.

9. Bake for about 15 minutes until risen, golden and firm to the touch.

10. Allow to cool slightly before removing from the tin.

11. Cool on a wire rack.

EILEAN DONAN CASTLE, DORNIE

SCOTTISH WEDDINGS

The Wedding Breakfast, as it is known in Scotland, is a true culinary experience. Food plays a vital role at all of our weddings.

Scottish weddings have a rich history, dating back to the Middle Ages. During this time, marriage was considered a sacrament and was overseen by the Church. Over time, weddings evolved to become elaborate celebrations that honoured family, friends and culture. They are a celebration of love, family and tradition.

Scotland has always been seen as a land of romance – and our more lenient marriage laws once enticed many young couples to elope to the Gretna Green Blacksmith Shop. Today, couples have the chance to be married over the exact same anvil by a blacksmith who moonlights as a priest.

Scotland has many unique wedding traditions, one of the most common being the wearing of the kilt, which has grown in popularity over the years. Another that I think is unique to Scotland is the scramble. I loved this as a kid. As soon as you saw a wedding car outside a church, you knew that your lucky day had come. As the newlyweds got into their car, the bride's father would throw handfuls of coins up in the air, and if you were really lucky the bride and groom would do the same. Wee kids would battle it out until every penny had been picked up.

'Tying the knot' is a very common term for getting married nowadays. It actually originated in Scotland. When people from different clans were getting married, they used some of their clan's cloth to tie them together into a knot.

In this chapter, I have included the types of recipes that I normally don't put in my books. They are slightly more in-depth and will require a bit of time to make. This is the sort of food that you would be making for a special dinner party. I have also included some dishes that I have made when catering for weddings over the years.

MINI CHEESE, ONION & SPINACH BRIDIES

This is my take on a Forfar bridie. I have taken the essence of a bridie and turned it into a little canapé that I actually serve at weddings. It's a great little technique – once you have figured it out, you can change the filling to whatever you wish.

According to legend, a baker from Forfar is credited with creating the first bridie in the 1850s. The pie might have been named after the tradition of serving it at weddings or after Margaret Bridie from Glamis, who sold them in Forfar's Buttermarket. The conventional recipe in Forfar involves using shortcrust pastry, whereas other areas of Scotland may use flaky pastry as an alternative.

MAKES 20 MINI BRIDIES

For the pastry
200g (7oz) plain flour
Good pinch of salt
100g (3½oz) butter, chilled
30ml (1¼fl oz) water
1 egg yolk, to glaze

For the filling
1 red onion
100g (3½oz) baby spinach, shredded
100g (3½oz) Cheddar-style cheese, grated
Cooking oil
Salt and pepper

For the pastry

1. Sieve the flour and the salt into a bowl.

2. Dice the chilled butter and add to the flour. Lightly rub together to achieve a sandy texture. Do this by running your hands down the insides of the bowl and go right to the bottom; when your fingers meet, slowly lift them out of the bowl, rubbing your thumbs over your fingers as you go. The secret of perfect pastry is to make sure you don't work it too much at this stage. I always try and make sure that I don't rub all the butter in completely. I like to see little flakes of butter once I have finished rubbing it in.

3. Make a well in the centre of the flour and butter, and add the water.

4. Gradually incorporate the water into the flour and carefully bring it together until you have a smooth paste.

5. Press into a flat round, wrap in cling film and allow to rest in the fridge for an hour before using. The reason you press the pastry into a flat round is so that you can pin it straight from the fridge.

For the filling

1. First, peel and slice the onion. Then, in a frying pan on a low to medium heat, heat a little oil and cook the onions until they start to soften.

2. Once soft, add the shredded spinach and cook for a few minutes until the spinach has wilted.

3. Allow the mixture to cool, then add the grated cheese. Season and put to one side.

To finish

1. Take your pastry from the fridge

and roll it out. Using a 7cm (2¾in) cutter, cut out disks. You can re-roll any pastry that is left.

2. Brush half of the edge of the pastry with the egg yolk.

3. Place a small amount of the mixture into the centre of each pastry disk. Fold over the pastry so that the edges meet perfectly, and make sure you expel as much air as possible before sealing up.

4. With the back of a slightly smaller cutter (5cm/2in), press and seal in the filling.

5. Next, take a crinkle cutter (6cm/2½in) and cut a new edge.

6. Brush with egg yolk and place on a tray.

7. Place them into a preheated oven at 180°C (350°F) for about 15 to 20 minutes.

KING SCALLOP

WITH BROWN CRAB, BARLEY AND SPINACH

This is a wonderful combination of shellfish, and is an ideal dish when entertaining friends and family. Most of the work can be done in advance and it's relatively quick to pull together. I have used this dish for many private dinners and events all over the world.

For the barley

50g (2oz) butter
1 shallot, finely diced
1 carrot, finely diced
3 cloves garlic, finely minced
200g (7oz) pearl barley, soaked overnight in water
150ml (5fl oz) white wine
400ml (14fl oz) shellfish stock
150g (5oz) crab meat, white and brown
Small bunch of spinach, shredded
Small bunch of chopped parsley
85g (3oz) Cheddar cheese, grated
Salt and pepper

For the scallops

4 king scallops
25g (1oz) butter
½ lemon
Small bunch of pea shoots, to finish

For the barley

1. Heat a saucepan, add half of the butter, then add the chopped shallot, diced carrot and minced garlic. Sweat for 3 to 4 minutes without colouring.

2. Add the soaked barley and cook for 2 to 3 minutes.

3. Pour in the wine and reduce until it has totally evaporated.

4. Start to add the stock a ladle at a time, making sure the previous ladle of stock has fully been absorbed.

5. Continue this method until all the stock has been absorbed and the barley is cooked.

6. Check the seasoning before adding the crab meat, spinach, cheese and parsley.

For the scallops

1. Make sure the scallops are clean and dry. Pan-sear on one side until golden brown.

2. Remove the pan from the heat and flip over the scallop.

3. Add the butter and a little squeeze of lemon juice.

4. Remove from the pan and serve with the barley.

5. Top with some pea shoots.

PAN-SEARED LANGOUSTINE

WITH COURGETTE, FENNEL, SAMPHIRE, TOMATO AND CITRUS BLACK PEPPER BUTTER

Langoustine is such a treat. They are one of Scotland's most famous exports – three-quarters of all langoustine come from Scotland. I was working in a fantastic restaurant in a beautiful town on the Ayrshire coast called Troon. The restaurant was next door to the harbour, where the main catch was langoustine. It was brilliant to watch the boats come in and really connect with the fisherfolk who provided the restaurant with this incredible product. Like most high-quality ingredients, you don't need to do much with them to make something special. This recipe is very simple to pull together. Once the langoustine is prepared, it's a very quick dish to cook.

- 20 medium langoustine
- 1 head fennel
- 2 courgettes, yellow or green
- 100g (3½oz) cherry vine tomatoes
- Small bunch of dill
- 1 lemon, juiced and zested
- 50g (2oz) samphire
- 50g (2oz) butter
- ½ tsp cracked black pepper
- Pinch of dried seaweed
- 1 tbsp good oil

1. To prepare the langoustine, bring a pan of salted water to a boil, add the langoustine and blanch for about 30 seconds. Remove from the pan and transfer to a bowl of ice-cold water.

2. Remove the head and claws, then carefully crack the shell on the tail to peel it away.

3. De-vein the tail by removing the black intestinal tract – you might have to score the top of the tail with a knife to remove it. Set the peeled tails aside for later. (You can keep the heads and the shells to make langoustine bisque. You can find that recipe on page 121.)

4. Thinly slice the fennel through a mandolin and cut the courgettes into long spaghetti strands. Cut the tomatoes in half and chop the dill.

5. Zest and juice the lemon.

6. You are now ready to cook the dish. In a large frying pan, add the oil and then the sliced fennel.

7. Cook on a medium heat until the fennel starts to soften.

8. Next, add the samphire and the courgettes, cook for 2 to 3 minutes until the samphire turns bright green.

9. Now, add the peeled langoustine and the halved tomatoes, this should only take a couple of minutes.

10. Lastly, add the butter, lemon juice and zest, cracked pepper, seaweed and dill. Serve.

PAN-SEARED SKATE WING

WITH CAPERS, OYSTER MUSHROOMS AND HAZELNUT BROWN BUTTER

Skate are caught all around the Scottish coastline. Some are incredibly large – one was caught a couple of years ago that was over 130kg (300lb). I have used skate wings over the years at lots of restaurants and people are always surprised that they taste so nice. Skate are a wonderful fish to cook and to eat.

The wings are made up of a thin spray of cartilage sandwiched with corrugated fillets, top and bottom, that are tender and delicious. The classic way of cooking them is with loads of butter and lemon.

25g (1oz) hazelnuts
150g (5oz) oyster mushrooms
4x 170g (6oz) portions skate wing
25g (1oz) flour
50g (2oz) butter
50g (2oz) capers
½ lemon, juiced
Small bunch of chervil
25ml (1fl oz) good oil
Salt and pepper

1. The first task is to chop and roast the hazelnuts. Pop them into a preheated oven at 180°C (350°F) until you start to see the skins come away from the nut. Remove them from the oven and place them into a clean tea towel. Bring the edges of the towel up into the shape of a money bag and rub the toasted nuts until most of the skins are removed. Chop and put to one side.

2. Take the oyster mushrooms and slice them into strips.

3. Next, season the skate and dust with flour.

4. Heat some oil in a large pan and place the skate wings in one at a time. Cook until the outside of the skate is golden brown.

5. Remove from the pan and place onto a tray. Put into the oven for 10 minutes until cooked.

6. Place the clams into a separate hot pan with a little oil, add the chopped shallot chopped dill and the white wine, and place the lid on top. Cook until the razor clams open (around 30 seconds) and remove and strain the cooking liquor.

7. Next, add the hazelnuts into the pan with the butter. Pop back onto the heat and cook the butter until it starts to go brown. Once you have a golden-brown butter, add the capers and a good squeeze of lemon juice. This will stop the cooking.

8. Finish with the chervil.

9. Put the cooked skate wings onto the plate and dress them with the mushrooms and the hazelnut and caper butter.

CONFIT DUCK LEG SALAD

WITH BUCKWHEAT, GRILLED ASPARAGUS & COURGETTE, LIME & HONEY DRESSING

This is a wonderful salad incorporating a couple of things that you have probably not used before. Confit duck is my favourite way of eating duck. I love that it is so versatile. Buckwheat is another ingredient that I think is underused – it is very good for you and is also easy to work with. Surprisingly buckwheat has no relation to wheat or any cereal; it is a seed from a plant that is closer to rhubarb than a grass.

This recipe also includes asparagus – Scottish asparagus is the best I have ever tasted, but it has a very short season (typically the end of April to June). It's worth seeking out when in season.

For the confit duck

- 1 tsp cumin seeds
- 1 tsp coriander seeds
- 3 juniper berries
- 50g (2oz) flaky sea salt
- 2 limes, zested (keep them for the juice used in the salad)
- 4 duck leg and thigh joints
- Bunch of thyme
- Sprig of rosemary
- 1 garlic clove, sliced
- 500g (1lb 2oz) duck fat (or enough to submerge the duck legs)
- 1 bay leaf
- 1 tsp black peppercorns

For the confit duck

1. First, make the spice mix and marinate the duck overnight (follow steps 2 to 5) the day before cooking.

2. Put the cumin and coriander seeds in a dry pan and toast until they are slightly coloured and aromatic.

3. Crush the toasted spices in a pestle and mortar. Crush the juniper berries and mix with the spices and the salt.

4. Zest the limes and mix with the spices.

5. Rub the mixture over the duck thighs, scatter with thyme, rosemary and sliced garlic, and chill for 24 hours, turning two or three times as they marinate.

6. Next day, heat the oven to 150°C (300°F).

7. Wipe the duck with kitchen paper and pat dry, but don't wash off the marinade.

8. Put the duck in a cast-iron casserole dish and cover it with the duck fat. You can top it up with cooking oil if needed.

recipe and ingredients continue on the next page

For the salad

200g (7oz) buckwheat groats
1 vegetable stock cube
500ml (2 cups) water
100g (3½oz) fine beans, trimmed
Bunch of asparagus, peeled and trimmed
1 courgette
200g (7oz) cherry tomatoes
50ml (2fl oz) honey
100ml (3½fl oz) good oil
2 limes, juiced
Handful mixed salad leaves
Salt and pepper

9. Add the bay leaves and peppercorns. Cover with foil and cook for about 2½ hours, or until the meat is almost falling away from the bone.

10. Allow to cool and put to one side. Once cool but not cold, remove the legs from the fat and pick off the meat, making sure you remove all the bones and any cartilage and put to one side.

For the salad

1. Add the buckwheat to a saucepan with the stock cube and water and bring it to a boil. Cover with a lid and reduce the heat to a simmer. Cook for 20 minutes.

2. Turn off the heat and allow it to stand for 5 minutes, then fluff with a fork and allow it to cool.

3. Meanwhile, in a separate pan, blanch your fine beans and asparagus in boiling, salted water for 60 seconds, then refresh in ice-cold water. This will help keep the vegetables bright green.

4. Slice the courgette and halve your tomatoes.

5. To make your dressing, combine the honey, oil and lime juice.

6. In a hot skillet or frying pan, sear the asparagus and courgette.

7. In a bowl, serve the vegetables and buckwheat, making sure everything is well combined.

8. Lastly, add the picked duck confit and tomatoes, and fold through the salad leaves. Season to taste.

9. Drizzle with your dressing and serve your warm salad immediately.

TWICE-BAKED MULL CHEDDAR SOUFFLÉ

WITH HAZELNUT, PEAR & PEA SALAD

I have a real love for the Isle of Mull. It's a place that has fascinated me since about the age of five, when I found out that Mull is the ancestral home of Clan Maclean. Fast-forward almost half a century and I was asked by the clan chief, Sir Lachlan Maclean of Duart, to host a thank you dinner for a group of people who had supported the restoration of Duart Castle. It was a real highlight of my career. The time spent with Sir Lachlan and his wonderful family is something I will never forget.

I was also lucky to spend a week living on the farm that produces Mull Cheddar. I was catering for a huge wedding at a castle in the north of the island and was able to book some rooms for my team. Mull is a special place and if you ever get a chance to visit you should.

This dish is a wonderful start to any meal, especially if you are cooking for friends. The beauty of it – and what makes it so special for a grand dinner like a wedding – is that it is very luxurious, and who isn't impressed when they see a soufflé on the menu? The other great thing about it is the fact that you can make it in advance and just heat it up as and when you need it.

- 50g (2oz) butter, plus extra for lining the mould
- 50g (2oz) plain flour, plus extra for lining the mould
- 500ml (2 cups) milk
- 1 bay leaf
- 200g (7oz) Mull Cheddar cheese, or cheese of your choice
- 4 egg yolks
- 4 egg whites
- 1 tsp Arran wholegrain mustard
- 1 tsp white wine vinegar
- 1 banana shallot, chopped
- 4 tbsp good oil
- 1 pear, cut into matchsticks
- 100g (3½oz) hazelnuts, roasted and roughly chopped
- Handful pea shoots
- 100g (3½oz) broad beans
- 200g (7oz) cherry tomatoes, halved
- Salt and cracked black pepper

recipe continues on the next page

1. Brush four ramekins with a little melted butter and dust with flour.

2. Shake out the excess flour and put the ramekins to one side for later.

3. In a saucepan, heat the milk and the bay leaf. Slowly bring it up to a simmer, then immediately turn off the heat.

4. Meanwhile, melt the butter in another small pan, then add the flour and mix to form a roux.

5. Cook out for 3 to 4 minutes, then slowly start to add the warm milk.

6. Stir continuously while milk is added until you achieve a smooth sauce with the consistency of thick double cream. If you add the milk a little at a time, you will avoid making a lumpy sauce.

7. Cook this out for 10 minutes over a very low heat to avoid burning the sauce, stirring every minute or so.

8. Remove from the heat and add 150g (5oz) of the grated cheese and the 4 egg yolks. Mix well, taste and season, if necessary. Cover the pan with cling film and put it to one side.

9. Preheat oven to 180°C (350°F).

10. Whisk the egg whites with a pinch of salt until soft peaks form.

11. Stir one-third into the cheese mixture to break it down.

12. Once the cheese mix has loosened, carefully fold in the remaining two-thirds of the whisked egg whites. You want to do this as gently as possible, and the key is not to knock out all the air from the whites.

13. Spoon the filling into the dishes until they are two-thirds full, then gently tap them on the table to remove any air bubbles.

14. Place in a shallow tray and pour in enough boiling water to come halfway up the sides of the dishes.

15. Bake for 20 to 25 minutes until set.

16. Once cooked remove the soufflés from the tray and refrigerate until cold. They will keep for a couple of days in the fridge.

17. When you are ready to serve the soufflés, preheat the oven to 200°C (400°F) and line a baking tray with non-stick paper.

18. Turn the soufflés out onto the tray.

19. Top each soufflé with the remaining 50g (2oz) of Mull Cheddar cheese and bake for 5 to 7 minutes.

20. To prepare the broad beans, remove them from their pods and boil them for 60 seconds, then cool immediately. Once cold, remove the outer shell.

21. Meanwhile, to make the pear and hazelnut salad, whisk the mustard and vinegar together in a bowl until combined.

22. Finely chop your shallot and add to the mustard mix.

23. Add some oil, whisking constantly until the dressing has emulsified.

24. Cut the pear into matchstick shapes. Roast and then chop the hazelnuts.

25. Combine the pea shoots, shelled broad beans, hazelnuts and pears in a bowl. Add approximately 2 to 3 tablespoons of the dressing, or enough to coat everything.

26. To serve, arrange the salad and the cherry tomatoes into your bowl and place the soufflé on top.

RAZOR CLAMS
WITH JERUSALEM ARTICHOKE AND SAMPHIRE

If you ever see razor clams at your local fishmongers, I encourage you to buy some and give them a go. They are sometimes known as spoots in Scotland. This recipe is a variation of the starter I did for the *MasterChef: The Professionals* final. Marcus Wareing said it was the best razor clam dish he had ever tasted and that it wouldn't look out of place in a three Michelin-star restaurant.

150g (5oz) Jerusalem artichokes
25g (1oz) butter
½ lemon, juiced
1 lemon
8 razor clams in the shell
1 fennel bulb
1 carrot
1 courgette
50g (2oz) samphire
2 shallots, chopped
50ml (2fl oz) white wine
Small bunch of flat-leaf parsley, chopped
Small bunch of dill, chopped
Small bunch of salad cress
Cooking oil

1. Begin by preparing the artichokes. Cut into very thin disks and fry in a little butter, with water and the juice of half a lemon, until cooked.

2. Peel and slice the lemon.

3. Rinse the razor clams in a bowl with running water to remove all grit.

4. Finely dice the fennel, carrot and courgette. Gently fry in oil until softened.

5. Add the artichoke disks and the samphire. Put to one side.

6. Place the clams into a separate hot pan with a little oil, add the shallots, dill and white wine, and place the lid on top. Cook until the razor clams open (around 30 seconds) and remove and strain the cooking liquor.

7. Boil the cooking liquor until it has reduced in volume by half and finish with a knob of butter and chopped parsley.

8. Finely slice the white flesh of the razor clams on the angle and add to the vegetable mixture.

9. To finish, place the vegetable mixture and sliced lemon into your dish, and spoon over some of the reduced cooking liquor.

10. Garnish with some salad cress and serve.

CRISPY OYSTERS
WITH OYSTER MAYONNAISE

Oysters are a wonderful ingredient. Nothing says celebration more than offering your friends and family an oyster at a special gathering. They are normally served raw and shucked to order; this recipe is a wee bit different, as the oysters are cooked. Some people don't like the idea of eating raw oysters. If you are daunted with trying to get the oysters open, you could ask your fishmonger to do it for you, or if you have a look online there will be loads of tutorials on how to open them.

15 oysters
250ml (8fl oz) water
50ml (2fl oz) vinegar
125g (4oz) plain flour, plus extra seasoned flour for coating
½ tsp baking powder
50g (2oz) cornflour
3 egg yolks
½ tsp Dijon mustard
½ tsp white wine vinegar
200ml (7fl oz) good oil
Pinch of salad cress or herbs, for garnish
Cooking oil for deep frying
Salt and pepper

1. Begin by opening the oysters. To do this, cover the oyster with a towel, leaving the hinged end exposed, and hold the oyster down firmly. Insert the oyster knife into the 'hinge' – this will take a bit of a push, but make sure the point of the knife is in the shell before you twist. Twist the knife to open the shell and cut under the oyster to release it. Give it a little sniff, as it should smell like the sea and be very pleasant.

2. Wash the shells and put them to one side.

3. Next, make the batter by adding the water and the vinegar to a bowl and sieving the flour, baking powder and cornflour together. The baking powder is going to give the batter a lift and the vinegar helps keep the batter crisp for longer.

4. Next, make the mayonnaise. Pop 3 of your oysters into a blender with your egg yolks, Dijon mustard and white wine vinegar.

5. Blitz together, gradually adding the good oil a little at a time (I use cold-pressed rapeseed oil, as I like its nutty, mild flavour and the colour is also nice).

6. Once made, double check the seasoning and put to one side.

7. Heat some oil in a pan to 175°C (345°F) and coat the remaining oysters in the seasoned flour and then the batter.

8. Carefully drop the coated oysters into the oil; they will only take a few minutes to cook.

9. Once they are golden brown, remove them from the oil and place them onto absorbent paper.

10. Season with a little salt and serve back in the cleaned shells. Top with a little cress to garnish.

LAMB & HAGGIS WELLINGTON

When I think of the word wellington, you might be surprised to hear I don't think of food, or even the boot, I think about traffic cones! The reason for this is one of Glasgow's most famous landmarks. There is a beautiful monument of the 1st Duke of Wellington astride a horse situated outside the Gallery of Modern Art. Since the 1980s this statue has had a traffic cone on its head. Over the years, the city council has tried everything to stop this, but as soon as one cone comes off, within hours a brand new one is in its place. It has become a cultural icon and a symbol of Glasgow.

This classic dish is a Scottish twist on the popular beef version, with succulent lamb loin and haggis. Wellingtons are often served at weddings in Scotland, but they are just as good for a cosy family dinner.

250g (9oz) loin of lamb, trimmed and fat removed
¼ savoy cabbage
2 eggs, for crêpe
50ml (2fl oz) milk
100g (3½oz) plain flour
250g (9oz) haggis
1 sheet puff pastry
1 egg, for glaze
3 sprigs of thyme, picked
Sprinkle of poppy seeds
Cooking oil

1. First, season the loin of lamb.

2. Heat some oil in a frying pan and place the meat into the pan with the sprigs of thyme. Sear the meat unil you have achieved a golden brown colour on every surface.

3. Next, blanch and refresh your cabbage leaves.

4. Your next task is to make a couple of French crêpes. This is a very easy thing to do: take two eggs, a splash of milk and a drop of oil, and whisk in enough flour until you get a thin batter consistency.

5. Taking a hot frying pan with a little oil, pour in some of the batter and swirl the pan until the mix creates a thin layer.

6. Cook the crêpe out in the pan and turn over, and repeat until you have two pancakes. For some reason, the first one you make is never that good; the second one is always better.

7. Overlap 2 to 3 sheets of cling film on a clean surface and lay down the two crêpes, slightly overlapping.

8. Spread the haggis on top of the crêpes.

9. Take some of your blanched cabbage leaves and dry them off using kitchen paper. Lay the cabbage on top of the haggis.

recipe continues on the next page

10. Place the lamb in the centre of the cabbage. Using the edge of the cling film, carefully wrap the crêpe, cabbage and haggis around the fillet of lamb.

11. Roll into a sausage shape, twisting the ends of the cling film on one side clockwise and the other anticlockwise to form a tight log. Chill in the fridge for 30 minutes to firm up.

12. On a lightly floured surface, place the pre-rolled puff pastry.

13. Unwrap your lamb log and lay it in the middle of the pastry.

14. Fold over the bottom half of the pastry and lightly brush the rest of the sheet with a beaten egg.

15. Roll the whole thing around the meat to encase it. Neatly trim the edges to create a parcel.

16. Transfer to a baking sheet and brush the pastry that is wrapped around the lamb with beaten egg and a generous sprinkle of poppy seeds.

17. Score the wellington with the handle of a teaspoon.

18. Chill for at least 30 minutes.

19. Preheat your oven to 200°C (400°F).

20. Bake for 25 to 30 minutes.

21. Remove from the oven and rest for 20 minutes.

22. Slice when ready and serve with your choice of vegetables and potatoes.

BRAMBLE CUSTARD TARTS

This is a wonderful combination of flavours. It can be adapted to work with the season and the occasion. It is a perfect dessert for a summer wedding, but the recipe will work with whatever soft fruit you can find if brambles are out of season. My kids cannot wait until the brambles are ready; we often go on long walks on summer nights and watch the progress of the berries. We have even mapped out where to find them and which ones will be ready for picking first.

MAKES 6 TO 8 TARTLETS

For the sweet pastry
200g (7oz) plain flour
125g (4oz) butter
Pinch of salt
1 egg, plus 1 to glaze
50g (2oz) caster sugar

For the custard filling
280ml (9½fl oz) double cream
Few drops of vanilla extract
Pinch of cinnamon
3 egg yolks
100g (3½oz) caster sugar

For the bramble jelly
4x 11cm (4⅓in) sheets gelatine
250ml (8fl oz) elderflower pressé
150g (5oz) brambles

NOTE:
You will need pastry rings and baking beans for this recipe. I have used 10cm (4in) rings, or you can use one large one.

For the sweet pastry

1. Rub the flour, butter and salt together until you have a breadcrumb texture. Make sure you can still see some small lumps of butter at the end of the rubbing-in process.

2. Crack the egg into a bowl and then add the sugar and lightly mix.

3. Add the egg and sugar mix to the flour and butter, and then using the palm of your hand bring this mixture together to form a dough. Make sure you don't overwork the dough at this stage.

4. Next, flatten out the pastry to form a disk about 3cm (1in) thick, wrap the pastry in cling film and place it into the fridge to rest.

5. Once rested, roll out the pastry until it's 2mm or 3mm (⅛in) thick. Next, cut circles about 4cm (1½in) wider than your pastry rings.

6. Carefully place the pastry over each ring, pushing it down inside until the pastry is the same shape as the mould.

7. You will find that you now have an overhang of pastry; you can bake it as it is, then trim the pastry once it's cooked. The advantage of this is you always get a finish that is nice and neat and to the top of the ring.

8. Place the lined rings into the fridge to rest for at least one hour.

9. Once rested, take your pastry-lined rings and cover them with a round of parchment paper. Preheat your oven at 180°C (350°F).

recipe continues on the next page

10. Put baking beans on top of the paper (alternatively, you could use dried pulses or rice), then place into the oven and bake until the edges start to colour.

11. Remove from the oven and let the pastry settle for a few minutes before you remove the baking beans and paper.

12. You will notice that the bottom of the pastry needs more cooking, but first you must create a waterproof barrier to ensure the pastry stays crisp even once you have put in your filling. To do this, break an egg into a bowl and glaze the pastry, making sure you cover it all.

13. Pop the pastry back into the oven and bake until it is evenly cooked.

14. You are now ready to pour in your custard mix and allow to it set.

For the custard filling

1. Place the cream, vanilla extract and a pinch of cinnamon into a thick-bottomed saucepan and slowly heat.

2. In a separate bowl, whisk the egg yolks and sugar together until the yolks lighten.

3. As the cream comes to the boil, add half of it to the egg yolk mix and then pour this mixture into the rest of the cream, and put it back onto the stove to thicken up.

4. You now have to be very careful – keep stirring the mix until it starts to thicken. It should resemble thin custard.

5. Once it coats the back of the spoon, pour the mixture into a large jug or bowl. This instantly stops the cooking.

6. Pour this mixture into your cooked tart cases and allow to set.

For the bramble jelly

1. First, bloom the gelatine. Do this by placing the gelatine into ice-cold water to soften it, then use a bowl big enough that you can submerge the sheets whole. Do not break them up.

2. Measure 50ml (2fl oz) of elderflower pressé into a small pot and bring to the boil.

3. Remove the gelatine from the cold water, making sure you squeeze out any excess water, and add the gelatine to the warm pressé.

4. Stir until it is melted, then add the remaining pressé.

5. Fill the jelly mould with halved brambles.

6. Carefully pour over the elderflower and gelatine mixture.

7. Place in the fridge until set.

To finish

Serve the bramble jelly on top of the custard tarts. I have used a set of ring moulds that work together perfectly. You can set the jelly in a tray and use a pastry cutter to cut the jelly to the size of your tartlet.

TORRIDON

HIGHLAND GAMES & FESTIVALS

HIGHLAND GAMES & FESTIVALS

Highland Games and Scottish festivals are a celebration of Scottish culture, tradition, music, dance and, of course, food. They are deeply rooted in the history of our country and showcase the talents and skills of the Scottish people. From tossing cabers and sheaf-throwing to the pipes and drums, sheepdog trials and Highland dancing, these games are a spectacle to behold.

But it's not just about the games. Scottish festivals offer a chance to experience the unique and mouth-watering flavours of Scottish cuisine: hearty stews and savoury pies; haggis, neeps and tatties. These dishes are a testament to Scotland's rich agricultural heritage, with locally sourced ingredients and time-honoured recipes passed down for generations.

The Highland Games have a rich history that dates back to ancient Scotland. Scottish warriors used to compete in physical contests to entertain their monarchs and demonstrate their strength and fitness. Over time, the games grew in popularity and became a staple of Scottish culture. In the late nineteenth century, they were formalised into organised competitions, and the first national games were held in Edinburgh in 1880. From then on, they became an annual event, attracting large crowds of spectators and competitors from all over Scotland.

As Scottish immigrants travelled across the globe, they brought their love of Highland Games with them. Today, Highland Games are held in many countries besides Scotland, including the United States, Canada, Australia and New Zealand.

The popularity of Highland Games has also led to the development of international competitions, such as the World Highland Games Championships, attracting elite athletes from all over the world, and the World Pipe Band Championships that are held at Glasgow Green in August every year and bring the very best bands together for an incredible competition.

Whether you are in Scotland, the United States or anywhere in between, the Highland Games are a great way to celebrate Scottish culture and heritage. I have been lucky to have experienced Highland Games all over the world – I am a regular visitor to the New Hampshire Games and also the Scottish Festival and Highland Games in Chicago. I have even been to the Alaska Highland Games! At the games I showcase Scottish food and culture, reciting stories and demonstrating traditional Scottish food for hungry audiences. In this chapter, I have selected a few recipes I have seen on my visits to games and festivals at home and abroad, and also some of the dishes I demonstrate live.

LANGOUSTINE BISQUE

This is a beautiful and delicate soup worth doing, especially since most people throw out the heads and shells from the langoustine. You might also be able to source the heads and shells from your local fishmonger for a small price. This recipe works just as well with lobster heads and shells.

MAKES 4 TO 6 PORTIONS

500g (1lb 2oz) langoustine shells
25ml (1fl oz) whisky
1 white onion
3 cloves garlic, chopped
2 sticks celery, chopped
2 carrots, chopped
3 tomatoes, chopped
1 tsp paprika
1 bay leaf
50g (2oz) flour
1 lemon, juiced
250ml (8fl oz) white wine
50g (2oz) tomato purée
1 litre (1 quart) water
50ml (2fl oz) double cream
2 tbsp good oil
Small bunch of chives, chopped
Salt and pepper

1. In a large saucepan, fry the langoustine shells in a little oil for 5 minutes. Add a splash of whisky.

2. Add the chopped onion, garlic, celery and carrot, and fry for a further 5 minutes. Add the chopped tomatoes, paprika, bay leaf and season. Stir well.

3. Dust the mix with the flour and stir again.

4. Add a squeeze of lemon juice, the white wine, tomato purée and 1 litre (1 quart) of water.

5. Bring to a boil and then gently simmer for 1 hour, skimming the surface periodically to remove scum.

6. Pass the contents through a fine-meshed sieve. Make sure you squeeze as much of the juice out of the shells as possible. There are loads of flavour in them, so it is worth taking a little time to do this.

7. Return the liquid to the saucepan, bring it to a boil, then turn down the heat and simmer for 30 minutes.

8. Gently whisk in the double cream, and double check your seasoning.

9. Divide the bisque into bowls and finish with a little oil and a sprinkle of chives.

CORNED BEEF BRISKET SANDWICH
WITH CARAMELISED ONION

Corned beef brisket is one of those dishes I always want to see at festivals and Highland Games. Scotland is renowned for its amazing beef, and brisket is an incredibly tasty and versatile cut. Despite how it looks, this recipe is relatively simple to make, even though it takes planning and time to brine it. One essential ingredient is the saltpetre; this is what keeps the beef nice and pink, even after it has been cooked. Saltpetre is easily purchased online.

I have suggested making this recipe with 2kg (4lb 6oz) of beef, as with the time and effort that goes into it, you want to have enough for a few days – indeed, a few dishes.

MAKES 4 PORTIONS; BEEF MAKES 12 PORTIONS

For the brine
100g (3½oz) brown sugar
60g (2½oz) sea salt
6g (1 tsp) saltpetre (potassium nitrate)
Small bunch of thyme
1 tsp allspice
1 stick cinnamon
¼ tsp red chilli flakes
1 tsp coriander seeds
4 cloves
1 tbsp black peppercorns
1 litre (1 quart) water

For the cooking of the beef
2kg (4lb 6oz) beef brisket
2 onions
2 sticks celery
½ leek
2 bay leaves

1. To make the brine, mix the sugar, sea salt, saltpetre, thyme and spices together in a saucepan with the water. Put on a medium heat and bring to the boil, then reduce the temperature and simmer for 5 minutes.

2. Set aside and allow to cool completely.

3. Meanwhile, remove any sinew and fat from the meat.

4. Pierce the meat with a metal skewer all over on both sides and place into a good quality food bag.

5. Pour the cooled brine over the brisket, then seal and store in the fridge for 5 to 7 days, turning the bag over each day.

6. When the brining time is up, remove the brisket from the bag and soak it in cold water for an hour.

7. Rinse the brisket well, then place it in a large saucepan and cover it with cold water.

8. Roughly chop the onions, celery and leek, then add to the pan with the bay leaves.

9. Bring to a boil, then reduce to a simmer and cook slowly for 2½ to 3 hours, or until the beef is tender.

10. Once cooked, allow the beef to cool in the water for about one hour. Carefully remove the beef to a chopping board and thinly slice off what you need.

For the sandwiches

2 large white onions

Few sprigs of thyme

4 crusty rolls or baguettes

100g (3½oz) smoked Cheddar cheese, sliced

2 pickled cucumbers, sliced lengthways

50g (2oz) French mustard

50g (2oz) butter, for spreading

50ml (2fl oz) cooking oil

To finish the sandwiches

1. Slice the onions thinly and place them into a large frying pan with a little oil and thyme, and cook on a low heat. Now and then stir the onions. It is going to take a little time for them to caramelise. Adjust the heat so that the pan always makes a little bit of noise.

2. In the meantime, prepare the rest of your ingredients and preheat your grill.

3. Cut your bread and spread the butter into the rolls, add the cheese and pop under the grill.

4. Once the cheese has melted, add the pickled cucumbers and the sliced beef. Top it with the caramelised onions and finish with a good drizzle of mustard.

LOBSTER & CRAB MACARONI
WITH SPINACH AND SMOKED CHEDDAR CRUST

This is a dish that I see at almost all the Scottish festivals and Highland Games I attend. It is a perfect case of opposites attracting. The homely dish of mac and cheese married to the king and queen of crustaceans works amazingly well. This is how you elevate a staple into a memorable dish.

300g (11oz) macaroni
25g (1oz) butter
2 banana shallots, finely chopped
3 red chillies, finely chopped
25g (1oz) plain flour
1 tbsp Dijon mustard
500ml (2 cups) milk
50ml (2fl oz) double cream
150g (5oz) smoked Cheddar cheese, grated
200g (7oz) lobster, cooked and chopped
100g (3½oz) crab meat
100g (3½oz) baby spinach
100g (3½oz) panko breadcrumbs
Small bunch of dill, chopped
Salt

1. The first job is to cook the macaroni in a large pot of boiling salted water for 12 minutes. Refresh in cold running water and leave to drain in a colander until needed.

2. Next, melt the butter in a small pan and add the chopped shallots and red chillies. Cook until soft without colour.

3. Add the flour to soak up any excess fat and create a paste. Add the mustard.

4. Slowly start to add the milk a little at a time until you have achieved a nice, smooth, glossy sauce.

5. Cook this out for at least 10 minutes, then add the cream to create a silky sauce.

6. Preheat your oven to 200°C (400°F).

7. Add the pasta to the sauce and then add half of the cheese. Next, add the chopped lobster and the crab meat and mix well.

8. Finish by adding the spinach. Mix it and let it wilt.

9. Pour the macaroni into an ovenproof dish.

10. Top with the remaining smoked Cheddar cheese and a sprinkle of breadcrumbs and place into the oven until the cheese has melted.

11. Add a sprinkle of dill and serve.

CHIPPY PICKLED ONIONS

Pickled onions are sold in fish and chip shops all over Scotland. You can find a few pickled offerings in chippies – pickled mussels are a real treat, and then there are pickled hard-boiled eggs . . . Not something I would go for, but people do love them.

I add a wee bit of spice to my pickled onions – it is not traditional, but I think it adds a lovely flavour. The use of honey also helps cut the acidity of the vinegar and adds a mellow sweetness.

1kg (2lb 4oz) pickling onions or small shallots
50g (2oz) salt
50g (2oz) sugar
500ml (2 cups) malt vinegar
200g (7oz) honey
3 cloves
1 tsp peppercorns
3 bay leaves

TO NOTE:
You will need 3x 500ml (16oz) jars for this recipe, or any sized jars with a combined volume of 1½ litres (1½ quarts).

1. Place the onions (just as they are, skins on) in a large bowl and cover with boiling water. Seal with cling film over the top.

2. Leave and allow to cool, then drain the water.

3. Trim the roots and tops, and then peel the onions.

4. Sprinkle the salt and sugar over the peeled onions, mix it all together and leave them overnight in the fridge.

5. Next day, rinse the onions well and them dry with kitchen paper.

6. Place the vinegar, honey, cloves, peppercorns and bay leaf into a large pan and heat slowly, just enough to dissolve the honey into the vinegar and infuse the flavours of the spices. It is important not to boil the mix at this stage.

7. Pack the onions into clean, sterilised jars.

8. Fill the jars with the remaining hot vinegar and spice mixture and check there are no air pockets. Seal the jars and leave them to cool.

9. The onions will be ready to eat after about 2 months, or they'll taste better if kept for 3 or more.

FISH SUPPER

If there is one dish I always see at Highland Games and Scottish festivals across the world it is fish and chips. It is a real classic and one of the most popular dishes in Scotland. That is why it is perfect when you are enjoying summer festivals that there is always a chippy van that will be producing amazing deep-fried offerings. I remember having wonderful fish and chips at the Alaskan Highland Games – they used a big chunk of halibut. In Scotland, it has to be haddock, and we serve it with loads of malt vinegar and chippy pickled onions. It is also served with lemon and tartar sauce in posher settings.

An important safety note: I suggest that if you are going to deep fry food at home, you do it in an electric fryer with a thermostat. Deep frying in a saucepan over a stove is lethal. You can pick up a decent fryer for under £20. Also note that homemade chips are amazing in an air fryer, and if you breadcrumb the fish, it also comes out amazing.

For the batter
400ml (14fl oz) beer or water
50ml (2fl oz) vinegar
250g (9oz) plain flour
100g (3½oz) cornflour
1 tsp baking powder
½ tsp salt

For the chips
1kg (2lb 3oz) potatoes, Maris Piper or Rooster (starchy potatoes are best)
Cooking oil for frying

For the fish
4x 200g (7oz) white fish fillets (I have used haddock)
Pinch of salt
200g (7oz) plain flour

For the batter

1. To make the batter, start by putting the beer (or water) and vinegar into a large bowl.

2. Next, gradually sieve the plain flour, cornflour, baking powder and salt into the beer and vinegar, whisking as you add. I find if you add the dry ingredients to the liquid, there will be less chance of it having lumps. The addition of the cornflour will help make the batter super crispy and the addition of the vinegar will keep the batter crispy longer. The baking powder adds lightness and bubbles to the batter. You might need to add a little more flour to get a nice coating consistency.

3. Once your batter has been prepared, put it to one side until needed.

For the chips

1. Peel and cut the potatoes into chips. The size is down to personal preference. Once cut, place the chips into a colander and rinse under cold running water.

2. Place the chips into a pot of cold water, add a good pinch of salt and put them onto the stove at a high heat and bring to a boil.

recipe and ingredients continue on the next page

For the tartar sauce

60g (2½oz) capers, chopped

60g (2½oz) gherkins, chopped

Few sprigs of dill, chopped

250g (8oz) mayonnaise

½ lemon

50g (2oz) caper berries to garnish

Salt and pepper, to taste

3. As soon as the water starts to boil, reduce the heat to a simmer and cook the potatoes until the point of a knife goes through them easily. The time depends on the size of the chips.

4. Drain them in a colander and allow them to steam out. Letting them air cool will help get rid of the excess water and they will cook much better and more safely, as water and hot oil are not a good mix.

5. To make the chips, place the potatoes into hot oil at 180°C (350°F). They should not take long to crisp up.

For the fish

1. Whilst the chips are cooking, you can prepare the fish. Season each fillet with a little salt, then place it into your flour and give the fish a good coat.

2. Place the fish into the batter. The idea is that the flour will stick to anything, and the batter will stick to the flour. Make sure that every part of the fillet is covered in the batter before adding it to the hot oil. The batter creates a protective seal around the fish and the fish inside the batter actually steams. If you have gaps, the oil gets into the fish and it is not as nice.

3. Deep fry for approximately 6 to 8 minutes, or until the batter is crisp and golden, turning the fillets from time to time.

4. Remove the fish from the oil once cooked and drain on some kitchen paper and season with a touch of salt.

For the tartar sauce

1. Chop the capers, gherkins and dill.

2. Add to the mayonnaise.

3. Finish with a little squeeze of lemon juice, and some salt and pepper.

4. To serve, garnish with caper berries.

To serve

Serve with a big wedge of lemon and some tartar sauce, or some chippy pickles and brown vinegar.

HOT SMOKED SALMON & CRAB FISHCAKES
WITH BROCCOLI SLAW

This is my take on an incredible lunch I had at the New Hampshire Highland Games at Loon Mountain. This was my first experience of a Highland Games in the USA, and I was completely blown away. I just could not believe its size and the number of people in attendance. I go back there every year and hold culinary demonstrations, showcasing Scottish food and traditions.

This recipe includes an ingredient I love: Old Bay seasoning. It comes from Maryland and is the perfect spice for this dish. If you ever go to Annapolis, you will find loads of amazing seafood shacks, and even before you go inside all you will smell is Old Bay seasoning.

For the fish cakes

500g (1lb 2oz) potatoes, peeled and cut into quarters
25g (1oz) butter
300g (11oz) hot smoked salmon
100g (3½oz) white crab meat
1 egg
50g (1oz) capers
Small bunch of chives, chopped
Small bunch of dill, chopped
15g (½oz) Old Bay seasoning
Salt and pepper

For the coating

100g (3½oz) plain flour, seasoned
2 eggs
Splash of milk
100g (3½oz) panko breadcrumbs

For the fish cakes

1. In a large pan, cook the potatoes. Cover them in cold salted water and slowly bring them to the boil.

2. Once cooked, drain the potatoes and allow them to steam out for a few minutes. Place them back into the pot and put it onto the stove on a low heat to dry them out further. Add the butter and then mash.

3. Before everything gets cold, mix the smoked salmon, crab meat, egg, capers, chopped chives and dill, and Old Bay seasoning, and check the seasoning. You might find that you will not have to add much salt to this, as the Old Bay and the smoked salmon will do a lot of the seasoning for you.

4. Once you are happy with the taste, shape the fishcakes. I do this by weighing out 100g (3½oz) balls of the mixture and then press them out into a pastry cutter. This gives the fishcakes a uniform size.

5. Place the shaped fishcakes into the fridge for an hour or so to firm up.

6. Once ready, coat them in breadcrumbs.

7. You will need three bowls – one with seasoned flour, another with the eggs and the milk, and lastly one for the breadcrumbs.

8. Roll the fish cakes in the flour, and then roll them in the egg and milk mixture, and then the breadcrumbs.

recipe and ingredients continue on the next page

For the broccoli slaw

1 head broccoli
50g (2oz) sugar
100g (3½oz) sultanas
2 tbsp white wine vinegar
2 red onions, sliced
200g (7oz) mayonnaise
50g (2oz) flaked almonds
100g (3½oz) cherry tomatoes, halved

9. You are now ready to cook them. You have a few options: you could deep fry them until golden; you could shallow fry them, making sure you keep them moving; or you could spray them with a little oil and bake them in a hot oven at 180°C (350°F).

For the broccoli slaw

1. Your first job is to prepare the broccoli. Start by cutting the broccoli into florets. With the broccoli stalk, peel the outside and discard, but keep peeling the stalk so that you get thin-cut strands, or if you have a mandolin cutter you could use that.

2. Next, take a large pan of salted water and bring it to a boil. Once it is boiling, add the broccoli florets and cook for 60 seconds, then add the cut stalk slices and cook for another 60 seconds.

3. Quickly drain and cool in cold running water. Once cold, put into a colander to get rid of any water. You will now have some bright green crunchy broccoli.

4. Slice the florets thinly.

5. In a separate bowl, combine the sugar, sultanas, white wine vinegar, sliced red onion and mayonnaise.

6. Mix this over the cooked, sliced broccoli to lightly coat.

7. Pop into a serving dish and top with the almonds and halved cherry tomatoes.

SLOW-COOKED PORK SHOULDER SANDWICH

WITH RED CABBAGE SLAW

If you have never tried to slow cook a pork shoulder, this is your chance. It is much easier than you think, and once you have made it, it will most definitely be a big hit with your friends and family. You will find this at almost every Highland Games or foodie festival anywhere in the world. However they make and serve it, you are guaranteed to have a stunning dish. Pork shoulder is an amazing cut; it is jam-packed with flavour.

MAKES 4 PORTIONS; PORK MAKES 8 PORTIONS

For the pork
1kg (2lb 3oz) pork shoulder, rind removed
25ml (1fl oz) good oil
1 tsp paprika
½ tsp chilli powder
½ tsp ground cumin
Pinch of salt
1 onion, roughly chopped
1 carrot, peeled and chopped
Small bunch of thyme
250ml (8fl oz) vegetable stock
3 tbsp brown sugar
1 bulb of garlic, halved through the circumference
4 buns of your choice, to serve

For the BBQ sauce
300ml (10fl oz) tomato ketchup
100g (3½oz) Dijon mustard
25ml (1fl oz) Worcestershire sauce
85ml (3fl oz) cider vinegar
85g (3oz) brown sugar
The cooking liquor from the pork

For the red cabbage slaw
¼ red cabbage, shredded
1 carrot, cut into matchsticks
1 tsp cider vinegar
200ml (7fl oz) crème fraîche
1 tsp honey

1. Preheat the oven to 130°C (250°F).

2. Take the pork shoulder and rub in the oil, then gradually rub in the spices, sugar and a little salt.

3. Place your cut vegetables, garlic and herbs into a deep roasting tray. Pop the pork onto the top of the vegetables, pour over the vegetable stock, cover the tray with a couple of sheets of tin foil and bake in the oven for 2 to 2½ hours, basting every 30 minutes or so.

4. Once cooked, carefully remove the pork from the tray and place it into a clean tray. Strain the cooking juices and put to one side to make the sauce. Using two forks, start to pull the meat apart.

5. For the BBQ sauce, combine the tomato ketchup, mustard, Worcestershire sauce, cider vinegar and brown sugar in a saucepan with the cooking liquor from the pork. Bring to a boil, then simmer until you have a coating consistency.

6. To make the slaw, combine the shredded cabbage with the carrot, cider vinegar, crème fraîche and honey, and mix well.

7. To serve, heat some of your BBQ sauce with the pulled pork, toast the buns, dollop a generous spoonful of pork into the buns and top with the red cabbage slaw.

SHORT RIB OF BEEF PASTRIES

A pastry pie is something that all cultures love. It is perfect for outdoor events, as it is hand-held and keeps you going as you enjoy the festivities. This recipe is my take on a pastry pie I had at the Scottish Festival and Highland Games in Itasca, Illinois. It was delightful and had a wonderful little hint of spice. These games are run and organised by the Chicago Scots, a group that I have had connections with for almost 25 years. Since 1845, the Chicago Scots have been working hard to promote Scottish culture and heritage throughout Chicagoland. Their principal charity is Caledonia Senior Living and Memory Care, and I am very proud to say that I have been able to spend some time there and cook for the residents.

MAKES 12 PASTRIES

500g (1lb 2oz) beef short ribs
1 onion, roughly chopped
1 tbsp chipotle paste
½ tsp smoked paprika
¼ tsp cayenne pepper
100g (3½oz) chopped tinned tomatoes
25g (1oz) tomato ketchup
25g (1oz) barbecue sauce
25ml (1fl oz) malt vinegar
25g (1oz) brown sugar
300g (11oz) puff pastry
1 egg yolk, for glazing
Flour for dusting

1. The day before, put everything but the ribs, pastry, flour and the egg yolk into a food processor and blitz to a sauce.

2. Put the ribs in a food bag, pour over the sauce and rub it all over. Marinate in the fridge overnight.

3. When you are ready to prepare the dish, preheat your oven to 140°C (275°F).

4. Tip the ribs and marinade into a deep tray, top with enough water to cover the ribs and then place foil over the top. Cook for 4 hours until tender.

5. Once cooked, remove the ribs from the tray, pour the cooking liquor into a pot and boil until the sauce is thick and reduced.

6. Once the beef is cool enough to handle, pull the meat off the bone. You should be able to pull it apart – if not dice it into even chunks – and mix it with some of the sauce.

7. You are now ready to build your pastries. You can do this in a few different ways, the simplest being the Cornish-pasty style. An alternative is a round pithivier-style pie.

8. To do this, dust the work surface with flour. Roll out the pastry to a thickness of ½cm (⅕in).

9. Cut circles out of the pastry 15cm (6in) in diameter, or whatever size you wish. You will need one circle of pastry per pie.

10. Place your circles of pastry onto the table and moisten the edge of the base with a little egg yolk to help the pastry stick.

11. Add the filling and fold over the pastry, making sure you get a tight seal.

12. You can use a crinkle cutter to finish them off, if you wish. Pop onto the tray and allow them to set in the fridge.

13. After an hour, remove from the fridge and brush the pastry with egg yolk to glaze.

14. Put them back into the fridge for 15 minutes.

15. Preheat the oven to 200°C (400°F).

16. Use a knife to make a small hole in the centre of the pastry and to score curved lines from the top to the bottom.

17. Bake in the oven for 15 to 20 minutes until golden and crisp.

WINKLES

Winkles are amazing and don't let anyone tell you differently. I am old enough to have fond memories of the mussel and whelk man coming around the streets in Glasgow in the late 1970s and early 1980s. I always got a little bag full of cooked winkles, folded over and secured with a pin. The pin was vital, as this was the tool used to pull the winkles out of their shell and eat them; it took a lot of persistence!

You are unlikely to see a vendor coming around the streets anymore, but they can be found at festivals and games all over Scotland. If you ever find yourself at the famous Glasgow Barras, you will find a great little seafood stall selling them alongside the unique clabby-doo mussel that is also worth a try. You can also forage your own. It is possible to collect winkles all year round. The picking takes place at low tide. I tend to only pick the ones that are secured on the rocks exposed by the retreating tide, as they are less likely to hold as much grit or sand.

1kg (2lb 3oz) live winkles
2 banana shallots, chopped
3 cloves garlic, minced
200g (7oz) mayonnaise
Small bunch of flat-leaf parsley, shredded
200ml (7fl oz) white wine
200ml (7fl oz) double cream
8 slices sourdough bread
Salt, 30g (1¼oz) per litre (quart) of water

1. Your first task is to purge the winkles. To do this, fill a small bucket with water and add enough salt so that it tastes like seawater – around 30g (1¼oz) of salt per litre (quart) should be enough. Submerge the winkles and allow them to soak for at least two hours.

2. Rinse them in plenty of cold running water and set to one side.

3. Meanwhile, chop the shallots.

4. Mix the minced garlic with the mayonnaise and half of the shredded parsley.

5. Place a large saucepan on the stove to heat it up.

6. In a bowl, mix the winkles with the wine and the shallots.

7. Next, drop everything into the hot saucepan: it should steam instantly, then carefully place a lid on the pot and cook at a high temperature for 4 to 5 minutes.

8. Turn off the heat and, with a slotted spoon, remove the winkles.

9. Next, add the double cream to the cooking liquid and bring to the boil, continuing to heat until the volume has reduced by half. This makes a flavoursome dipping sauce for your bread.

10. Serve your guests the winkles in the shell with a pin or an opened-out paper clip, and the bread and dipping sauce, and garlic mayonnaise on the side.

GRILLED LOBSTER

WITH CABBAGE, CELERIAC & APPLE SLAW

This is the type of dish that you will find at many festivals around Scotland in the summer months. It reminds me of the kind of food you eat from seafood shacks in coastal towns – in fact, these shacks were the inspiration for my own seafood restaurant, Creel Caught. Lobster is such a treat, a luxurious ingredient, but it is worth the effort and the price. You will be able to pick up a live lobster from your local fishmongers, but, as with most things, you can actually get live lobsters delivered to your home.

2x 600g (1lb 5oz) lobsters
50g (2oz) salt
½ savoy cabbage, shredded and blanched
¼ head celeriac, cut into matchsticks
1 apple, cut into matchsticks
¼ cucumber, sliced
4 spring onions, sliced
100g (3½oz) mayonnaise
1 lemon, juiced and zested
Bunch of dill, chopped
50g (2oz) butter

1. Your first task is to pop your lobsters into the freezer for about 20 minutes. There are two reasons for this: first, we do not want the lobster to suffer; second, the lobster goes to sleep in the cold air; if they are asleep when cooked they give you much better and more tender meat, as they do not tense up when hitting the water.

2. Choose a large pot to cook the lobster in. Fill with water to three-quarters full and bring to a simmer, adding about 50g (2oz) of salt.

3. Now add lobsters to the pot and cook at a gentle simmer for 5 to 6 minutes.

4. Take off the heat and remove the lobsters.

5. Once cool, split the lobster in half lengthways and crack the claws to make it easier to gain access to the meat.

6. Clean out the head cavity, making sure you get the sack out from behind the eyes and also remove the waste track that runs down the tail.

7. Remove the meat from the tail, thinly slice it and pop it back in place. Put to one side.

8. To make the slaw, mix the shredded and blanched cabbage, celeriac, apple, cucumber and spring onions with mayonnaise.

9. Add the zest of half a lemon and a squeeze of lemon juice to the mix, and finish with chopped dill.

10. To reheat the lobster, chop up the butter and evenly distribute it over the meat. Next, pop it under a hot grill or on the BBQ for a few minutes until it is hot.

11. Serve with your slaw and a wedge of lemon.

ARDVRECK CASTLE, LOCH ASSYNT

THE GLORIOUS TWELFTH

THE GLORIOUS TWELFTH

The Glorious Twelfth is the term used to describe the opening day of the shooting season for red grouse in Scotland, which falls on 12 August each year.

The tradition of grouse shooting dates back to the nineteenth century and has long been associated with the aristocracy and landed gentry. Grouse shooting became popular in the Highlands of Scotland in the 1850s and gradually spread to other areas of the country.

The Glorious Twelfth has become something of a cultural event in Scotland and is celebrated with a range of traditional foods. One of the most famous dishes associated with the day is roast grouse. This is typically served with game chips, bread sauce and redcurrant or blackcurrant jelly. Other traditional foods that are often enjoyed on the Glorious Twelfth include pheasant, partridge and venison.

It is a huge time in the hospitality industry as well, especially in five-star hotels and fine-dining restaurants. The race to get the first of the grouse onto the table is still fought out. Stories of Scottish grouse being raced the length of the UK to the tables of restaurants in the hotels of Park Lane in London still resonate with me.

In Scotland, the season kicks off with all the shooters in their kilts. The sound of bagpipes adds to the excitement.

This was also a significant time in my career, as I worked in a Cook School in Kilmarnock run by Braehead Foods, which are one of the main dealers and processors of feathered game in the UK. The whole place would come alive – there would be an extra 60 or 70 staff employed during the game season. They would process game that would end up on tables around the world. It is also worth mentioning that all the game in this book was provided by Braehead Foods, using game picked up at local shoots.

PAN-SEARED LOIN OF VENISON

WITH CAULIFLOWER, BROCCOLI, CARROT PURÉE, ROSTI POTATOES AND A ROOT VEGETABLE & BARLEY SAUCE

Venison is a healthy and delicious meat and is becoming more popular and easier to get. Since I started cooking in the 1980s, venison has changed dramatically from being a dark and very strong gamey-flavoured meat (which, between you and me, I thought was borderline inedible most times). Over the decades in Scotland the systems in place for getting the deer off the hill and on to the plate have been drastically improved. This means that the animal is not hanging as long. As a result, we have a much better product that is easier to find and is not as strongly flavoured, therefore more people are being won over by it. You can pick venison up now in good supermarkets and butcher's shops. This dish has a lot of different elements; most can be made in advance reheated when needed.

For the venison

4x 150g (5oz) venison loin
2 sprigs of rosemary
2 sprigs of thyme
2 cloves garlic
25g (1oz) good oil
25g (1oz) butter
Small bunch of pea shoots, to garnish

For the sauce

1 carrot
2 stalks celery
½ leek
1 white onion
½ bulb garlic
2 sprigs of rosemary
2 sprigs of thyme
1 litre (1 quart) brown chicken stock
50g (2oz) barley, soaked and cooked
25g (1oz) good oil
25g (1oz) butter

For the venison

1. Begin by marinating portions of venison in a little oil and half the herbs.

2. When needed, sear the venison in a hot non-stick pan with the remaining half of the herbs and two slightly crushed garlic cloves. Add the butter and finish in the oven at 180°C (350°F) for 4 to 6 minutes, depending on size.

4. Allow the meat to rest before cutting.

5. Serve with the carrot purée, rosti potato, cauliflower and broccoli. Finish with the pea shoots.

For the sauce

1. Cut half of the vegetables roughly and place into a pan with the oil and slowly caramelise.

2. Once you have achieved good colour on the vegetables, add the garlic and the herbs and then add the stock.

3. Cook for 40 minutes, then strain the liquor into a wide-bottomed pan.

4. Cut the other half of the vegetables into fine dice, then reduce the liquor with the vegetables and cooked barley.

5. Once you have reduced this by two-thirds, whisk in the butter.

recipe and ingredients continue on the next page

For the carrot purée

500g (1lb 2oz) carrots
25g (1oz) butter
Salt and pepper

For the rosti potatoes

500g (1lb 2oz) potatoes (Maris Piper or Rooster work well)
85g (3oz) butter
Salt and pepper

For the cauliflower

½ cauliflower
2 sprigs of rosemary
2 sprigs of thyme
½ bulb garlic, chopped
50g (2oz) butter
1 sheet silicon paper (cartouche)

For the broccoli

300g (11oz) tender-stem broccoli
25g (1oz) butter
Salt and pepper

For the carrot purée

1. To make a carrot purée, wash, peel and rewash your carrots, then dice and place into a pot of seasoned water.

2. Bring to the boil and cook until tender.

3. Pass through a colander, making sure to keep any liquid.

4. Place the carrots and butter into a blender and purée until smooth. You may need to add a little of the liquid to get the correct consistency.

5. Season to taste.

For the rosti potatoes

1. Peel and grate the potatoes.

2. Using a fresh tea towel, place a handful of the grated potato into the cloth, bring up the corners to make a money pouch shape, then twist and squeeze out the liquid.

3. Meanwhile, melt the butter, add to the potatoes with salt and pepper, and mix.

4. The mixture should come together as the butter sets.

5. To cook the rosti, place small amounts into a hot frying pan – you can use a scone cutter, if you are looking to create perfect circles.

6. Once you have cooked each rosti in the pan, put it to one side until you are ready to finish them: roast them in the oven at 180°C (350°F) until crisp.

For the cauliflower

1. Break the cauliflower into florets. Cut each floret in half and place flat side down in a non-stick pan.

2. Add the herbs, garlic and the butter.

3. Cover with a disk of greaseproof paper – this helps keep the steam in and will ensure the cauliflower slowly cooks through as it caramelises.

For the broccoli

1. Bring a pot of salted water to the boil, add the broccoli and cook for 1½ minutes.

2. As soon as it turns bright green, remove from the water and immediately cool in cold water.

3. When needed, reheat in a pan with the butter and season with salt and pepper.

POT ROAST PHEASANT

WITH BARLEY ROOT VEGETABLES AND HISPI CABBAGE

I would say pot roasting has all but gone from the family cooking repertoire, replaced with the advent of the slow cooker. I much prefer the higher temperatures of pot roasting; I think you get a better result. Pheasant is a perfect candidate for this method of cookery, as it is a very lean meat and can otherwise dry out very easily. Like a lot of game, it is now much easier to find. Most local butchers will be able to get it for you, and some local markets and farmers' markets will also stock them in season.

For the pheasant
2 carrots
2 sticks celery
12 baby onions
1 leek
300g (11oz) mushrooms
1 pheasant, oven-ready
50g (2oz) plain flour, seasoned with salt and pepper
50ml (2fl oz) cooking oil
2 rashers smoked streaky bacon, thinly sliced
3 cloves garlic, peeled and crushed
4 sprigs of thyme
1 bay leaf
100g (3½oz) barley, soaked in water until soft
100ml (3½fl oz) Marsala or red wine
50ml (2fl oz) whisky
150ml (5fl oz) chicken stock

For the cabbage
1 hispi cabbage
50g (2oz) butter
½ tsp chilli flakes
Salt and pepper

1. Prepare the vegetables. Peel the carrots and cut them in half, then cut each half into quarters. Next, peel the strings off the celery and then cut each stick to a similar size as the carrots.

2. Peel the baby onions and leave them whole. Slice the leeks lengthwise and then chop and thoroughly wash.

3. Clean and prepare the mushrooms. Keep them separate from the other vegetables.

4. Preheat your oven to 160°C (325°F).

5. Dust the pheasant with half of the flour, then heat the oil in a frying pan.

6. Brown the pheasant all over, then remove it from the dish. This will add loads of flavour and also make it look amazing.

7. In the same pan, fry the bacon, vegetables, garlic and herbs with the remaining 25g (1oz) of the seasoned flour.

8. Cook until the vegetables start to colour, then pour everything into a saucepan big enough that it will hold the pheasant.

9. Add the soaked barley.

10. Put the pheasant on top and pour any of the juices back in. Pour on the Marsala (or red wine), the whisky and the stock, then cover and cook for 1 hour 20 minutes to 1 hour 40 minutes, or until the leg meat comes away easily.

11. Next, prepare the cabbage. Cut it into quarters and then cut the quarters in half so that you end up with eight equal wedges.

12. Heat a frying pan. Add butter and, once foaming, add the wedges of cabbage.

13. Cook until golden, about 8 to 10 minutes, turning the cabbage as it colours.

14. Halfway through the cooking, sprinkle with the dried chilli flakes and season with salt and pepper.

15. Once cooked, remove from the pan and keep warm. In the same pan, cook the mushrooms, then add them into the pot with the pheasant for the last 10 minutes of cooking.

16. Once the pheasant is cooked, carefully remove it from the pot and serve it with the vegetables and bacon. You will also have a wonderful sauce in the pot.

17. I would serve this dish family style, with everything in the middle so people can help themselves.

ROAST MALLARD CONFIT LEG

WITH MASHED POTATOES, PLUM CHUTNEY AND BABY CARROTS

Mallard is a wild duck that is very common in Scotland. It has a delicious, gamier flavour than domesticated duck . The hunting season lasts from 1 September to 31 January. The legs on wild duck tend to be tougher, and the only way I have found to utilise them is to cook them long and slow. It is vital that you do not overcook the breast meat; it has to be cooked pink. If you have never had confit duck legs before, you are in for a real treat. They are magical, though they take a little bit of time, but I think it is worth it.

MAKES 4 PORTIONS; GRAVY MAKES 10 TO 12 PORTIONS; CHUTNEY MAKES 10 PORTIONS

For the confit leg
- 4x mallard leg and thigh joints, taken from the birds
- 25g (1oz) flaky sea salt
- 2 oranges, zested
- A few sprigs of thyme
- 1 sprig rosemary
- 1 garlic clove, sliced
- 1 bay leaf
- 250g (9oz) duck fat, or enough to totally submerge the duck legs
- 1 tsp black peppercorns

For the crowns
- 2 mallard crowns
- 2 carrots, chopped
- 1 onion, roughly chopped
- Sprig of rosemary
- Small bunch of thyme
- 8 to 10 baby carrots
- 25g (1oz) butter
- 25ml (1fl oz) good oil
- Salt and pepper

For the confit leg

1. The first task is to remove the legs from the bird. To do this, pull the leg away from the body and carefully score the skin between the body and the leg. Once cut, pick up the bird and pull the leg back on itself until you pop the ball joint out – you should hear a pop! Once the ball joint is out, cut the leg away from the body. Repeat on the other legs.

2. Next, zest the orange and mix it with the salt.

3. Rub the mixture over the four mallard legs, scatter with thyme, rosemary and sliced garlic, and chill for 24 hours, turning two or three times as they marinate.

4. Next day, heat oven to 150°C (300°F).

5. Wipe the legs with kitchen paper and pat dry, but don't wash off the marinade.

6. Put the mallard in a small, deep tray and cover it with the duck fat. You can top it up with vegetable oil, if needed.

7. Add the bay leaf and peppercorns. Cover with foil and cook for about 2½ hours, or until the meat is almost falling away from the bone.

8. Allow to cool and put to one side. Once cool, but not cold, remove the legs from the fat and pick off the meat, making sure you remove all the bones and any cartilage and put to one side.

recipe and ingredients continue on the next page

For the roast gravy

1 tray natural juices (bones and vegetables from the roast)
1 glass red wine
25g (1oz) tomato purée
2 tbsp plain flour
1 litre (1 quart) brown stock (the pouch ones work well for this)
2 sprigs of thyme
2 sprigs of rosemary
Small bunch of chives, chopped

For the mashed potatoes

400g (14oz) potatoes
25g (1oz) butter
25ml (1fl oz) milk
Salt

For the plum chutney

250g (9oz) white onions, chopped
500g (1lb 2oz) plums, stoned
2 cloves garlic, crushed
½ tsp mixed spice
200g (7oz) soft brown sugar
50ml (2fl oz) cider vinegar
Small bunch of thyme
1 sprig of rosemary
½ tsp salt
½ tsp cracked black pepper

For the crowns

1. You should be left with two crowns of mallard; they will need a little work before we can roast them. You will need to remove the bottom half of the carcass. You do this by taking your knife down through the carcass where the legs were and remove the overhanging bit of bone. Trim the wing bones as well.

2. Once you have removed the carcass, chop it into two or three pieces and place it alongside the chopped carrots and onion, rosemary and thyme, and put it in the fridge for later.

3. Next salt the bird inside and out. It is advised that you leave the bird overnight, as this will help tenderise the meat.

4. Before roasting the mallard, make sure you have the mashed potato, confit legs and chutney made.

5. To roast the crowns, take a large frying pan and add a little oil. Pan-fry the meat, skin side down until you have achieved a golden-brown colour. Next, add the chopped carcass and the chopped vegetables and colour them also.

6. Meanwhile, pre-heat your oven to 200°C (400°F).

7. Pour the browned vegetables and the carcass into a roasting tray, place the crowns on top, and roast for 18 to 25 minutes. You are looking to cook the mallard crowns to a core temperature of 53°C (127°F) to keep the meat nice and pink and tender.

8. Once cooked, remove from the oven and allow to rest for at least 10 minutes. Keep the tray to one side for your gravy.

9. Whilst they are resting, you can make your gravy and cook the baby carrots.

10. Place the carrots in a small pan with a little butter and oil. Slowly cook until they are softened, then season with salt and pepper.

For the roast gravy

1. Using your roasting tray from the cooking of the crowns, pop the tray onto the heat, making sure you keep all the chopped vegetables, herbs and cooking juices from the crowns. You are looking to caramelise the vegetables and lift the flavour off the bottom, making use of what was left from your roast.

2. Next, add about half of the wine – use the wine to help unstick what's at the bottom of the tray.

3. Then add the tomato purée, then the flour, and work into the mixture. This might start to clump together, but don't worry.

4. Add the rest of the wine and bring the whole lot to a boil.

5. Lastly, add the brown stock and whisk the whole lot together.

6. Transfer the mixture into a thick-bottomed pan and reduce until you have the required flavour.

7. The more you reduce the sauce, the stronger the flavour will be, and the thicker it will become.

8. Once you are happy with the thickness and the flavour, add your chopped chives.

For the mashed potatoes

1. I feel the secret to great mashed potatoes is following some very simple rules. Make sure you use the correct potato (Maris Piper, King Edward or Desiree). Peel the potatoes with a potato peeler and not a knife, as you will save putting loads of potato in the bin. Don't cut the potatoes up too small for cooking, as they tend to break up and make the mash watery and starchy.

2. Place the potatoes in a deep pan, cover with cold water and a pinch of salt, and bring to a boil slowly. Don't keep stabbing them with a knife; again, it breaks them up.

3. Once the water comes to a boil, turn it down to a simmer and cook until tender.

4. Drain the potatoes in a colander and allow them to steam out for a few minutes. Place them back into the pan and dry out over a low heat.

5. Now mash until smooth, then add butter and milk, making sure you do not allow the potatoes to cool down.

6. I think the best way to mash them is through a potato ricer, or a mouli grater makes the job easy and provides you with lump-free mash. It saves loads of time.

7. Season to taste.

For the plum chutney

1. Your first job is to wash, peel and rewash the onions, then finely chop them.

2. Next, wash the plums and carefully cut through the centre, twist and remove the stone. Cut each half into four.

3. Place your chopped plums and onions into a large pan.

4. Add all the other ingredients.

5. Slowly bring to a boil, stirring the whole time. Once it comes to a boil, lower the heat so that the chutney cooks at a simmer.

6. Make sure you stir the chutney regularly, and make sure it does not catch and burn.

7. Keep on cooking until the chutney is thick and sticky.

8. A good way to check if it is cooked is to draw your wooden spoon across the chutney. If the space that is left fills up with runny liquid, the chutney is not ready yet.

9. Remove any thyme and rosemary stalks.

10. Once cooked, cool and put to one side.

To finish

1. Once the birds have rested, carve the two breasts off each bird and run your knife down the centre line on the top of the mallard. Put to one side.

2. Heat the mashed potatoes, place the picked confit duck legs into a small saucepan, add a little of your gravy and heat up.

3. Spoon some mashed potato onto the plates, a spoonful of the chutney and then the baby carrots, and top with the roast mallard breasts and confit duck. Finish with your gravy.

ROAST PARTRIDGE

WITH CARROT & APPLE PURÉE, CARROTS AND BABY TURNIPS

There are two different types of partridge available in Scotland, grey-legged and red-legged. The latter was introduced into the UK in the eighteenth century. It is similar in appearance to the grey-legged partridge, but it has a distinctive reddish-brown coloration on its legs. The grey-legged partridge, also known as the common partridge, is a native bird of Scotland. It has a distinctively grey-brown plumage and a short, curved beak. The grey-legged partridge is smaller than the red-legged variety, and is often found in farmland and open grassy areas. Like most game birds, they are easy and quick to cook. Most partridge these days are hand-reared and managed for the sport of shooting.

For the vegetables
100g (3½oz) baby turnips
400g (14oz) carrots
25g (1oz) butter
Salt and pepper
Few sprigs of thyme

For the carrot purée
500g (1lb 2oz) carrots
1 tsp curry powder
1 green apple, diced
25g (1oz) butter
Salt and pepper

To cook the partridge
2x oven-ready partridge
25g (1oz) butter
1 onion, chopped
Small bunch of thyme

For the vegetables

1. To prepare the vegetables, wash and halve the baby turnips, and peel and cut the carrots into batons. In a small pan, add the butter and enough water to cover the carrots and turnip halves. Add a pinch of salt and a few sprigs of thyme.

2. Place onto the stove and bring to a boil. Reduce the heat and simmer until the vegetables are cooked.

For the carrot purée

1. Wash, peel and rewash the carrots, then dice them and place into a pot of seasoned water.

2. Add the curry powder, butter and bring to a boil and cook until almost done. Then add the diced apple and cook until the carrots are ready.

3. Pass through a colander, making sure to keep any liquid.

4. Place carrots and apple into a food processor and blitz until super smooth. Add more liquid as you need it.

5. Season to taste and keep warm.

To cook the partridge

1. Preheat the oven to 200°C (400°F).

2. Rub the skin of the partridges with a third of the butter and season with salt and ground black pepper.

2. Place the butter, the chopped onion and half of the thyme inside the bird's cavities.

3. Next, pop the birds into the oven for 20 to 25 minutes. Once cooked, allow to rest for 10 to 15 minutes before cutting.

4. Once the partridge has rested, cut it through the middle and serve it with the carrot purée and vegetables.

ROAST GROUSE

WITH MUSHROOMS, KALE, BABY BEETROOT, MUSHROOM PURÉE AND ROAST POTATO

When I think of the Glorious Twelfth, I think of grouse – often referred to as the King of Game Birds. The red grouse is unique to Britain and is mostly found in Scotland; the shooting season runs from 12 August until 10 December. Shooting became very popular in Scotland in the 1870s. We have been managing the habitat for grouse ever since. The management of the land and the eradication of pests from its environment ensure there is a plentiful stock of this much-prized bird. Grouse is the gamiest of all the game birds, in my opinion. It is very flavoursome – it gets the strong flavour from its diet, which is predominantly heather.

50g (2oz) butter
500g (1lb 2oz) chestnut mushrooms
2 shallots, finely chopped
1 garlic clove
6 sprigs of thyme
1 bay leaf
85ml (3fl oz) chicken stock (a cube will work for this)
2 tbsp crème fraîche
1 tsp truffle oil, optional
4 large potatoes
150g (5oz) baby beetroot
2x grouse crowns
200g (7oz) kale
50ml (2fl oz) good oil
Salt and ground black pepper

1. For the mushroom purée, melt half the butter in a medium to high sided pan over a medium heat.

2. Add 300g (11oz) of the mushrooms and cook, stirring occasionally, until browned and the liquid is evaporated, usually about 6 to 8 minutes.

3. Add the shallots, garlic, two sprigs of thyme, bay leaf and stock, bring to a simmer and cook until the stock is reduced by half – about 8 to 10 minutes.

4. Discard the thyme and the bay leaf, and transfer the mixture to a blender. Add the crème fraîche and the truffle oil (optional), and purée until smooth. Season with salt and pepper.

5. Preheat the oven to 180°C (350°F).

6. For the roast potatoes, cut the top and bottom off the potatoes and, using an apple corer, cut out 12 cylinders. (The remaining potato can be mashed).

7. Place the potato cylinders onto a tray with a little splash of oil and two sprigs of thyme, and season with salt and pepper. When needed, cook until the centre of the potato is cooked.

8. For the beetroot, pop it into a small tray, drizzle with oil and two sprigs of thyme, and season with salt and pepper.

9. For the grouse, season the crowns inside and out with salt and ground black pepper.

10. Preheat your oven to 220°C (425°F).

11. Heat the oil in an ovenproof frying pan over a high heat, add the grouse, skin-side down, and fry for 1 to 2 minutes, then turn and fry on the other side for 1 to 2 minutes, or until the grouse is golden-brown on all sides.

12. Transfer the grouse to the oven for 10 to 12 minutes, or until cooked to your liking. Remove the grouse from the pan and cover it with foil to rest.

13. Next, quarter the remaining mushrooms, place into a hot pan and cook until golden, add the shredded kale and season with salt and pepper. Finish with the remaining 25g (1oz) of butter.

14. Finally, pop your potatoes and beetroot into the oven to reheat, warm the mushroom purée up in a small pan, carefully carve the breasts off the grouse and slice. Serve with the potatoes and the vegetables.

CLASSIC ROAST WOODCOCK

WITH CABBAGE, SMOKED BACON AND ARRAN MUSTARD

Woodcock is a rare and stunning game bird. I have never been on a shoot, but I did work for a company that processed the birds from the shoots and we only got a few birds a week through the door. I have only cooked these birds on a few occasions and have never had them on a menu. It is a real luxury to be able to cook and showcase them in this book.

I have written this recipe for four, but the reality is that woodcock are so difficult to shoot, you will be lucky to get four birds. You can adapt the recipe to the number of birds you manage to get a hold of.

4 oven-ready woodcock
4 slices bread
50g (2oz) butter
1 savoy cabbage
50g (2oz) Arran wholegrain mustard
Bunch of chives, chopped
12 rashers dry-cured bacon
2 sprigs of thyme
2 sprigs of rosemary
3 cloves garlic
100ml (3½fl oz) port or red wine
300ml (10fl oz) brown stock
1 tsp flour
25ml (1fl oz) oil
Salt and pepper

NOTE:
Woodcock is a unique bird. It is traditionally cooked with its inners still inside and its head still on; in fact, its beak is used to truss the legs together. I have gone middle ground on this recipe – I have kept the innards in, but I have removed the head.

1. The first thing is to sort the woodcocks. Make sure you remove as many of the feathers as possible.

2. Preheat the oven to 180°C (350°F).

3. Heat some oil in a frying pan. Once hot, sear the woodcocks with the herbs until the outside is golden brown.

4. Next, pop them onto a tray and bake in the oven for 15 to 20 minutes. Allow the birds to rest once they have been removed from the oven.

5. Meanwhile, take a large scone cutter and make a circle from each slice of bread. Pan-fry the bread in 25g (1oz) of butter until golden brown.

6. To prepare the cabbage, remove the outer leaves and discard them (these leaves are normally very dark and sometimes damaged). Cut the root off and start to remove the leaves; you will be able to take off most of them before you get to the centre. With each leaf, remove the centre spine and discard it.

7. Shred the leaves by rolling them up tightly and running your knife through them as thinly as you can.

8. With the centre core, quarter it and shred it – there is no need to remove the centre spine, as the centre is very tender.

9. Blanch the shredded cabbage in boiling water for 60 seconds, then refresh in cold water.

10. Cut your bacon into thin strips and pan-fry until cooked. Add the blanched cabbage, chopped chives and the wholegrain Arran mustard, and mix well.

11. The next job is to remove the legs and the breasts from the woodcock.

12. Put the legs and breasts to one side, then remove the innards of the birds into a small pan.

13. Chop the carcass and put it in the same pan. Next, add the port and reduce by half, sprinkle in the flour and then add the stock.

14. Cook until the sauce coats the back of a spoon.

15. Sieve the sauce and put it to one side.

16. To serve, place the fried bread onto the plate, topped with the cabbage and bacon, then arrange the two breasts and legs onto each plate.

17. Dress the plate with the sauce and serve.

PAN-SEARED FILLET OF COD
WITH CURRIED MUSSEL & CRAB BROTH

Cod is a large, round fish that is a popular game species for sport fishermen who are deep-sea fishing around the coasts of Scotland. Cod is a magnificent fish to eat and work with – you will be able to find it in good fishmongers. Like all fish, it is actually simple to work with and is easy to cook. The main thing to remember is not to overcook it. I use cod loads, as it works well in fine-dining restaurants and casual dining alike. I even used it in my main dish when I was in the finals of the Young Chef of the Year.

1kg (2lb 3oz) mussels
175ml (6fl oz) white wine
1kg (2lb 3oz) potatoes
100g (3½oz) spinach, shredded
Small bunch of flat-leaf parsley, finely chopped
100g (3½oz) cherry tomatoes, halved
4 shallots, chopped
150g (5oz) smoked streaky bacon
2 cloves garlic, crushed
1 tsp curry powder
100ml (3½fl oz) double cream
4x 150g (5oz) cod fillets
100g (3½oz) peas
100g (3½oz) crab meat
Cooking oil

1. First, prepare and steam the mussels. To do this, rinse them in cold running water and remove the beards and any big barnacles.

2. Place a saucepan onto the stove on a high heat.

3. Meanwhile, drain the mussels into a bowl and add the white wine.

4. Pour the mussels into the hot pot. Quickly place the lid on and let the mussels cook until they open – this should only take a few minutes.

5. Once cooked, remove from the heat and drain the mussels in a colander over a large bowl. Make sure you retain the cooking liquor, as this will be the base for your broth.

6. Next, peel the potatoes and dice them into 1cm (½in) cubes. Shred the spinach and the parsley, and halve the tomatoes.

7. Chop the shallots and bacon, and crush the garlic.

8. Pick the cooked mussels from the shells, discarding any that do not open, and put them to one side.

9. In a clean pan, heat a little oil. Add the bacon and the chopped shallots, and cook until the bacon is crisp. Add half a teaspoon of curry powder and the garlic.

10. Next, add the diced potatoes and the cooking liquor, and simmer until the potatoes are almost cooked.

11. Add the double cream and bring to a simmer.

12. Next, sprinkle the cod fillets in a little of the curry powder and pan-fry until they are firm to the touch.

13. Meanwhile, add the spinach, tomatoes, peas, parsley and crab meat to the sauce. Gently cook until the spinach has wilted.

14. Serve in bowls with your pan-fried cod on top.

SCOTTISH GAME PIE

This type of pie is called a raised pie; the pastry is a very traditional hot water paste. I find these types of pies very satisfying to make and they always impress. The technique remains the same regardless of the filling. You could ask your butcher to make the filling for you as I am sure they will have a game pie mix to hand. The great thing with this recipe is that once you have made one, your mind will start racing to what pies you can make next. From a historical point of view we have been eating pies like this since the Roman times, always reserved for grand occasions on the tables of the great and good, filled with all sorts of outlandish ingredients including swan. They say the unofficial national dish of Fife is a game pie filled with wild rabbits; it is called the Kingdom of Fife pie.

MAKES 3 SMALL PIES, OR ONE LARGE 6 TO 8 PORTION PIE

For the hot-water pastry
225g (8oz) plain flour
50g (2oz) bread flour
35g (1¼oz) butter
50g (2oz) lard
½ tsp salt
100ml (3½fl oz) hot water

For the filling
400g (14oz) mixed game meat (venison, pheasant, rabbit)
100g (3½oz) pork belly, minced
50g (2oz) streaky bacon, diced
1 large onion, chopped
2 cloves garlic, minced
Small bunch of flat-leaf parsley, shredded
1 tbsp Worcestershire sauce
125ml (4fl oz) beef stock
1 bay leaf
1 egg yolk, beaten for egg wash
Salt and pepper, to taste

TO NOTE:
I would make the filling first, as the pastry works best when rolled whilst it is still hot.

For the hot-water pastry

1. Sift the plain and bread flours together with the salt.

2. Next rub in the butter and lard until you have a sandy texture.

3. Add the boiling water and mix well with a spoon.

4. Once it has come together, get the dough out onto the table and knead it until it becomes smooth and pliable.

For the filling

1. Preheat the oven to 200°C (400°F).

2. Heat a frying pan over medium heat and cook the chopped onion and minced garlic until the onion becomes translucent. Allow to cool.

3. Cut the game meat into small pieces and season generously with salt and pepper.

4. Place the game into a bowl, and add the minced pork belly, the streaky bacon and shredded parsley.

5. Add the Worcestershire sauce, and beef stock. Mix until well combined.

6. Roll out two-thirds of the paste and line a deep pie dish with it. I have used 3 mini 10cm (4in) spring form baking tins.

7. Cut a circle big enough to line your chosen tins or pie moulds.

8. Fill the pastry with the meat mixture until it reaches the top of the mould or dish.

9. Roll out the remaining third of the hot water paste to create a top crust for the pie (or pies).

10. Place it on top of the pie and crimp the edges to seal.

11. Cut a small hole in the centre of the top crust to allow steam to escape.

12. Brush the top of the pie with the beaten egg yolk.

13. Bake the pie for 20 minutes at 200°C (400°F) and then turn the oven down to 160°C (325°F) for 30 minutes, or until the crust is golden brown.

14. You can serve the game pie hot or cold.

DATE & WALNUT BREAD

This is a delicious recipe. It's a bit of an all-rounder as it can work with many things, it eats well with both sweet and savoury additions, and it is perfect for picnics and days out. I have even included this bread on cheese boards and meat platters.

MAKES 1 LOAF

125g (4oz) butter, plus extra for greasing the tin
200g (7oz) dates, pitted and roughly chopped
½ tsp bicarbonate of soda
150ml (5fl oz) boiling water
150g (5oz) light-brown sugar
2 eggs
1 tsp baking powder
225g (8oz) self-raising flour
150g (5oz) walnuts, roughly chopped
1 tbsp icing sugar
Pinch of salt

1. Begin by preheating your oven to 160°C (325°F). Take a 900g (2lb) loaf tin (23x13cm/9x5in and 7cm/3in deep) and grease it with butter and line it with baking parchment.

2. In a large bowl (a stand mixer would be helpful), add the butter (cubed and softened) along with soft, pitted dates that have been roughly chopped. To this, add bicarbonate of soda and boiling water, allowing it to stand for around 25 to 30 minutes until the dates have softened.

3. Whisk in the light-brown sugar until you get a smooth consistency, then gradually whisk in two eggs until everything is combined.

4. Beat in the baking powder, self-raising flour, and a pinch of salt until there are no lumps of flour left and everything is smooth. Fold in 100g (3½oz) of roughly chopped walnuts, before pouring the mixture into your prepared tin. Finally, sprinkle the remaining 50g (2oz) of chopped walnuts over the top.

5. Bake for 20 minutes and then turn the oven down to 150°C (300°F). Continue cooking for 45 to 50 minutes until the cake is a lovely golden brown.

6. To test if it is cooked, insert a metal skewer into the centre of the cake. If it comes out clean, it is ready.

7. Allow the cake to stand in the tin for 15 minutes; this allows it to settle.

8. Transfer it to a cooling rack to cool it completely.

9. Finally, dust with icing sugar lightly over the top, then cut into slices and serve.

RASPBERRY PUDDING

This is a brilliant time of year to go raspberry picking; from August to early October, Scotland is full of wild brambles and raspberries. This lovely traditional recipe will help use up the abundance of fruit that I am sure you will find. You can use shop bought but it's more fun getting out and finding your own.

MAKES 4 TO 6 PORTIONS

For the filling
150g (5oz) raspberries
50g (2oz) caster sugar
Pinch of cinnamon
½ lemon, zested

For the topping
50g (2oz) butter
50g (2oz) caster sugar
1 egg
125g (4oz) self-raising flour
100ml (3½fl oz) milk
Pinch of ground cinnamon
1 lemon, zested
Pinch of salt
50g (2oz) icing sugar, to dust at the end

For the filling

1. Place the raspberries into a saucepan with the sugar, cinnamon, and lemon zest.

2. Place the pan onto a medium heat with a lid on until the juice from the fruit starts to run.

3. Remove the pan from the stove and take off the lid. Allow it to cool.

For the topping

1. Place the butter and the sugar into a large bowl and beat until it is light and fluffy.

2. Beat in the egg a little at a time, then add the flour, milk, cinnamon, lemon zest and a pinch of salt.

3. Pour your raspberry mixture into a pudding dish and spread the topping smoothly over the top.

4. Preheat your oven to 180°C (350°F) and bake the pudding for 25 to 30 minutes until the sponge is cooked.

5. Finish with a light dusting of icing sugar.

MACHRIE MOOR STANDING STONES, ISLE OF ARRAN

HALLOWEEN

Halloween, or Samhain as it was historically known in Scotland, has been celebrated for centuries as the Celtic New Year. It was believed that on this night, the boundary between the worlds of the living and the dead became blurred and spirits could cross over into the mortal realm.

In Scotland, the celebration of Samhain involved lighting bonfires and offering food and drink to the spirits. It was also customary to disguise oneself in costumes to confuse and ward off any malicious spirits that might come through the veil.

With the influence of Christianity, All Hallows' Eve was eventually combined with All Saints' Day and All Souls' Day and became known as Hallowmas. This led to the tradition of guising, children going door-to-door, dressed in costumes and asking for treats, which is now a popular practice in Scotland and many other countries.

Additionally, the carving of turnips into lanterns with scary faces became a beloved Halloween tradition in Scotland and is still practised today; however, you are more likely to find a carved pumpkin than a turnip.

Halloween in Scotland is now more influenced by North America than its own past. Each year it becomes bigger and bigger. People's homes are decorated with all sorts of spooky decorations, as hundreds of kids swarm the streets knocking on doors, trick or treating.

In this chapter, I have tried to focus on food you can make that would be a special treat for those little kids who will no doubt be knocking on your door come 31 October.

BAKED BUTTERNUT SQUASH

WITH MUSHROOMS, BUTTER BEANS AND CLAVA BRIE

I think this is the perfect family-friendly dish as it is a fun way to introduce kids to different flavours. You can place the baked squash in the middle of the table so people can help themselves. I have always found if kids can make their own choices from a table of food, they tend to eat more especially if their peers are enjoying it.

2 small butternut squash
200g (7oz) mushrooms, chopped
100g (3½oz) butter beans, cooked
4 spring onions, chopped
50g (2oz) Clava Brie, or any soft cheese you like
50g (2oz) baby spinach, shredded
25ml (1fl oz) good oil
Microgreens
Salt and pepper

1. Preheat your oven to 190°C (375°F).

2. Cut the butternut squash in half and remove the seeds. This will create two bowls that we will stuff with the other ingredients.

3. Using a small knife cut deeply into the squash and create diamond shapes.

4. Drizzle with oil and season with salt and pepper. Pop into the oven for 30 to 40 minutes until the squash is soft and cooked.

5. Meanwhile, in a large frying pan, cook the mushrooms with a little oil. When almost cooked add the cooked butter beans, spinach and spring onions. Season with salt and pepper.

6. Once the butternut squash is cooked, scoop out the cooked flesh and add to the mushroom mix.

7. Stuff each butternut squash with the vegetable mixture, making sure to pack it firmly, so everything fits in nicely.

8. Top the stuffed butternut squash with 50g (2oz) of Clava Brie, or any other cheese of your preference.

9. Place the butternut squash halves on a baking sheet and bake for 15 to 20 minutes until everything is nice and hot and the cheese has melted into the filling.

10. Once removed from the oven, allow the dish to cool for a few minutes before garnishing with microgreens on top.

APPLE FRUSHIE

Frushie is an old Scots word meaning 'brittle' or 'crumbly' which applies to pastry. Who doesn't love an apple pie? This variation has the addition of honey and rose water. Be careful when using rose water: if you use too much it can taste more like an air freshener rather than a dessert. This is a tasty treat that couldn't be more of the season.

For the pastry
200g (7oz) plain flour
125g (4oz) butter
50g (2oz) caster sugar
2 eggs
Pinch of salt

For the filling:
5 Braeburn or Cox apples
2 tbsp honey
85g (3oz) sugar
Few drops of rose water

1. Rub the flour, butter and the salt together until you have a breadcrumb texture. Make sure that you can still see some small lumps of butter at the end of the rubbing-in process.

2. Crack one egg into a bowl, then add the sugar, and lightly mix.

3. Add the egg and sugar mix to the flour and butter, then using the palm of your hand bring this mixture together to form a dough. You are looking for the dough to still have traces of butter visible, this is an indication that you have not overworked it.

4. Next, flatten out the pastry to form a disk about 3cm (1in) thick.

5. Cling film the pastry and place it into the fridge to rest.

6. Once rested, roll out thinly and line a 20cm (8in) tart case, making sure you leave some pastry to finish the pie.

7. Peel, quarter and remove the core from the apples.

8. Slice the apples thinly and start to line the pastry case with them, adding a little honey, sugar and rose water to each layer until you reach the top. Save a little of the sugar to sprinkle on at the end.

9. With the remaining pastry, roll it out thinly and cut it into strips. Next, start to lay the pastry into a lattice design on top of the pie.

10. Preheat your oven to 180°C (350°F).

11. Beat the remaining egg. Brush the pie with a little layer of beaten egg and a sprinkle of caster sugar.

12. Bake in the oven for 25 to 30 minutes until it is golden brown.

BARLEY SUGAR

Barley sugar is a very traditional sweet, particularly in Scotland where it has been produced for hundreds of years. This recipe might reintroduce your friends and family to a bygone era. Just like any sugar-boiling recipe be very careful as molten sugar can cause very bad burns. This is the perfect old-fashioned sweetie that you could make and give out to the ghosts and superheroes that will be ringing the doorbell on 31 October.

50g (2oz) barley
600ml (2¾ cups) water
400g (14oz) granulated sugar
2 lemon zest strips
1 tbsp lemon juice

NOTE:
You will need a sugar thermometer or temperature probe and a non-stick silicone mat for this recipe.

1. Your first task is to make the barley water. To do this add your barley to the water and bring it to a boil and then gently simmer until the barley is soft. You will need to top the water up as you go.

2. Once the barley is soft and you still have liquid in the pan let it cool and settle.

3. When the barley cooking liquor is cool, sieve off 300ml (1¼ cups) of the water into a clean heavy-bottomed pan.

4. Add the sugar into the pan with the barley water and cook on a medium heat until the sugar dissolves. It is important not to stir at this point.

5. Meanwhile, using a vegetable peeler take two full-length strips of zest from the lemon and add to the sugar and barley water mix in the pan.

6. Increase the heat of the stove to high and bring to a boil.

7. You will find that the sugar mix will bubble and splash up onto the sides of the pan. Take a clean pastry brush and a cup of cold water, and using the wet brush clean the sides of the pan with it to get rid of any sugar crystals that might form.

8. Boil gently, without stirring, until the syrup reaches the soft-ball stage at 115°C (240°F).

9. Add the lemon juice and boil until the syrup reaches the hard-crack stage of 150°C (300°F) on a sugar thermometer or temperature probe.

10. Dip the pan in a bowl of ice water to stop the cooking and dry the sides of the pan.

11. Remove the lemon zest.

12. Pour the mixture onto a non-stick silicone mat and let it stand for a few minutes.

13. Using the edges of the mats, fold the sugar mix into itself until it is cool enough to pick up. Be very careful at this stage as the sugar might have molten hot spots in the middle.

14. Pick up the lump of sugar and start to pull and fold the sugar onto itself, to even out the temperature.

15. Start to pull long strands from the lump and, as you pull, twist the sugar to obtain the classic barley sugar twist shape.

16. Using oiled scissors, cut into individual sweets.

17. Let the sweets harden. Store in an airtight container.

CANDY APPLES

Candy apples are a bit of fun. I have found when making these that the smaller the apple the better. Getting your teeth into a candy apple is not easy, especially if you are a child. Another tip is to use flat lollipop sticks as it stops the apples from spinning around as you try to bite into them. Having a temperature probe or sugar thermometer really helps with this recipe. Also, be careful as the sugar gets extremely hot and it can be very dangerous if it splashes on your skin.

MAKES 8 APPLES

8 small apples
600g (1lb 5oz) caster sugar
4 tbsp golden syrup
1 tsp lemon juice
150ml (5fl oz) water
½ tsp red food colouring
8x lollipop sticks

1. The first task is to wash and thoroughly dry the apples. You might find that the apples have a waxy coating; if so, you will need to dip each apple into boiling water for a few seconds to get rid of the wax.

2. Next insert the lollipop sticks so that they are firmly positioned in the apples.

3. Put the apples to one side on a baking sheet lined with greaseproof paper, coated with cooking spray if you have it.

4. Combine the sugar, golden syrup, lemon juice and water in a heavy-bottomed saucepan over a medium heat.

5. Bring it to a boil and cook the mixture until your thermometer reaches 150°C (300°F), the hard crack stage. If you do not have a thermometer, test the sugar by dropping a small amount into cold water. It should harden instantly and, when removed, be brittle – hence 'hard crack'. If it's soft, continue to boil.

6. Remove the sugar mixture from the heat and carefully stir in the red food colouring.

7. One by one, carefully dip the apples into the sugar mixture, swirling to coat them thoroughly. Allow any excess to drip back into the pan. I find if you can prop up the pan at an angle so that you reduce the surface area of the sugar it will stay hotter longer. If the sugar cools and the coating becomes too thick, pop the mix back onto the heat.

8. Transfer the coated apples to the prepared baking sheet and allow them to cool until the sugar has fully hardened.

CINDER TOFFEE

Cinder toffee, or honeycomb as it is sometimes known, is not only a Scottish childhood memory – but there's also a very similar treat in most cultures. When I think about cinder toffee my first thoughts are of a chef and friend of mine, Jacqueline O'Donnell, who has made cinder toffee her go-to demo dish. We were once working together on an event at the Edinburgh Fringe called Dinner in the Sky. Dinner in the Sky was an outdoor dining experience just beside Edinburgh Castle. We had a table with room for 16 diners that was suspended 100 feet up on the end of a huge crane. I was the host and Jacqueline was the guest demo chef of the day. She decided to do her signature cinder toffee 100 feet up, just inches away from the guests who were strapped into their seats. When I saw the mix starting to boil out of the pan it was one of the scariest moments of my career.

MAKES 8 TO 10 PORTIONS

25g (1oz) butter
400g (14oz) caster sugar
200g (7oz) golden syrup
22g (2 tsp) bicarbonate of soda
Cooking oil

1. Your first job is to prepare a baking tray: take a sheet of greaseproof paper and lightly coat it with a little bit of oil.

2. Push the paper, oiled side up, into the tin.

3. Put the butter, caster sugar and golden syrup into a deep saucepan over a gentle heat until everything has melted. Make sure you are using a large pan as the mix is going to expand a lot.

4. Do not let the mixture boil until the sugar grains have disappeared, as this will cause the whole mix to crystallise.

5. Once completely melted, turn up the heat slightly and simmer until you have a lightly coloured caramel.

6. Turn off the heat, tip in the bicarbonate of soda and beat in with a wooden spoon until it has all disappeared and the mixture is foaming.

7. Very carefully scrape the mixture into your prepared tin.

8. The mixture will continue to bubble in the tin. Put it to one side until it cools.

9. Once cool you can break it into chunks and enjoy.

10. You can use cinder toffee in loads of different ways, from ice creams to coating in chocolate and cheesecakes; the list is endless.

FLY CEMETERY CAKE

(FRUIT SLICE)

This is a fun and easy cake to make; it is also appropriate for Halloween. This creation can be found all over Scotland. I know it as dead fly cake but it is more commonly known as fly cemetery cake. It is still as popular now as it has ever been.

For the sweet pastry

125g (4oz) butter
200g (7oz) soft flour
1 egg
50g (2oz) caster sugar
Pinch of salt

For the filling

100g (3½oz) brown sugar
50g (2oz) butter
1 red apple, peeled and grated
3 tsp mixed spice
200g (7oz) currants
200g (7oz) raisins
50ml (2fl oz) milk, for brushing the pastry
50g (2oz) caster sugar, for dusting once it is out of the oven

TO NOTE

You will need a 30x20cm (12x8in) baking tin.

For the sweet pastry

1. Rub the butter, flour and the salt together until you have a breadcrumb texture. Make sure that you can still see some small lumps of butter at the end of the rubbing-in process.

2. Crack the egg into a bowl, then add the sugar, and lightly mix.

3. Add the egg and sugar mix to the flour and butter and then using the palm of your hand bring this mixture together to form a dough. You should have a smooth pliable dough that you should still be able to see little flakes of butter through.

4. Next, cut the pastry in half and flatten out each half of the pastry to form a disk about 3cm (1in) thick.

5. Wrap the pastry in cling film and place it into the fridge to rest.

For the filling

1. To make the filling, put the sugar and the butter into a pan, place onto the stove, and on a low heat melt the two ingredients together. Once melted, add the grated apple and the mixed spice, currants, and raisins.

2. Mix and allow it to cool before assembly.

3. Preheat the oven to 170°C (335°F).

4. Once the mixture is cold, roll out one-half of your pastry big enough to line the bottom and sides of your baking tin.

5. Next pour in your filling and spread out evenly with the back of a spoon.

6. Roll out your second half of the pastry and layer on top of the mix. Cut away any spare overhanging pastry.

7. Brush with milk, and with the point of a knife pierce in a couple of places to create steam vents. This will ensure a crisp pastry.

8. Pop into your preheated oven for 30 to 45 minutes.

9. Once golden brown, remove from the oven and dust with caster sugar.

10. Cut into your desired shape whilst it is still warm.

HIGHLAND TOFFEE

Growing up in Scotland in the eighties every kid loved Highland toffee. It is a wonderfully sweet and chewy treat. I have great memories of it, especially the Highland cow on the wrapper. If you are going to attempt this recipe, it comes with a health and safety warning. This mixture gets extremely hot and if any of the mixture gets on your skin you are in trouble. I always suggest you have a large bowl of water, or a sink filled with water, just in case you splash any of the mixture onto your hand. This will give you a very quick way of cooling it and avoiding a serious burn.

450g (1lb) caster sugar
250ml (1 cup) double cream
75g (3oz) butter, cubed

1. Line the base and sides of a 20x30cm (8x12in) baking tin with baking parchment. A good tip is to brush the sides of the tin with a little oil, and this will help hold the paper in place.

2. Put the sugar into a large, heavy-bottomed, deep pan.

3. Pop onto the stove and heat gently, stirring occasionally until the sugar has melted.

4. Once it has come to a boil, keep a close eye on it.

5. Boil the sugar, without stirring, until you get a deep caramel colour.

6. Once you have the rich colour, add the cream and butter. Be careful as this will create a lot of steam.

7. Once the mix has come back to a boil, cook for 2 to 3 minutes.

8. Carefully pour your molten toffee into your prepared tin.

9. To ensure you have a nice level top on the toffee lift the tray off the surface and drop it; this will knock out any bubbles and also settle the toffee.

10. Allow to cool. After 2 to 3 hours the toffee should be cold enough to cut.

11. Use the baking parchment to lift the set toffee out of the tin, then cut the block into squares. If the toffee is sticking to the knife, lightly oil the blade. Wrap the toffee pieces in waxed paper. Store in a jar for up to two weeks.

PLUM, CINNAMON & HONEY TARTS

This is a brilliant and very easy recipe. Plums are super tasty and work well at this time of year. It is one of those recipes that can have a big impact without needing hours of work. It is also a great recipe to get the kids involved with as there are loads of things for little hands to do.

MAKES 6 TO 8 TARTS

6 plums
320g (11oz) pre-rolled puff pastry
50g (2oz) honey
85g (3oz) brown sugar
1 tsp ground cinnamon

1. Your first task is to halve the plums, remove the stone and then slice the plums as thinly as you can.

2. Next unwrap and roll out your pastry and cut 4cm (1½in) strips from the longest side of the roll.

3. Brush the strips with honey and then dust with brown sugar and cinnamon.

4. Lay one strip of pastry at a time and place the slices of plum on the top half of the pastry, on top of each other like a fan, until you get to the end of the pastry.

5. Once you have done that, fold the bottom half of the pastry over to meet the top half of the pastry. You should have the plums sticking out the top.

6. Now carefully roll the pastry up into a spiral.

7. Next place the roll into a muffin tin.

8. Repeat for the other tarts.

9. Preheat your oven to 180°C (350°F).

10. Once you have completed all the tarts, place them in the oven for 18 to 20 minutes.

11. Remove from the tin before going completely cold, as they will set in the tin once cold.

JAM ROLY POLY

Childhood memories flooded back to me as I prepared this delicious jam roly poly recipe. I remembered sitting in the school dinner hall eagerly awaiting dessert, and the excitement that came with spotting the light and fluffy jam roly poly. Now, as an adult, I still adore this classic dessert. I hope they are still making them in schools.

MAKES 12 SLICES

75g (3oz) self-raising flour
75g (3oz) caster sugar
3 eggs
150g (5oz) raspberry jam
Cooking oil for greasing

1. To begin, preheat the oven to 200°C (400°F).

2. Lightly brush the base of a 33x23cm (13x9in) tin with cooking oil.

3. Cut a sheet of greaseproof paper to fit the base of the tin with a good overhang and brush the paper with a little more oil before dusting with caster sugar and flour.

4. Whisk the sugar and eggs with an electric mixer for 10 minutes until pale and thick enough for the mixture to leave a trail when the whisk is lifted.

5. Sift half of the flour into the mixture and fold in carefully until no traces of flour remain.

6. Repeat with the remaining flour, taking your time to do it gently.

7. Pour the mixture into the prepared tin and use a spatula to smooth it evenly into the corners. Bake in the oven for 10 to 12 minutes, until golden and risen and just firm to the touch.

8. While the sponge is baking, loosen the jam by stirring it well in a separate bowl.

9. Lay out a damp clean cloth on the work surface and lay a piece of greaseproof paper that is larger than the sponge on top.

10. Run a knife around the edge of the warm sponge and turn it out onto the paper.

11. Peel the paper off the base of the sponge and trim off the edges. Spoon the jam onto the sponge and spread it out, leaving a little border of clean sponge all around.

12. Use the paper to help you roll the sponge tightly, and sit it seam-side down until it has cooled. Once cooled, slice and serve for a delicious and nostalgic treat.

OATIE SCONES

Scones originated in Scotland in the early sixteenth century. They are still very popular and can be found in cafés, tearooms, and bakeries all over Scotland. Oatie scones are a wee bit different, the mixed spice and cinnamon give this scone a grown-up feel. I think these works best slightly heated with a good dollop of butter in the middle. Alternatively, you could get them strung up and dipped in honey, and have the kids try to grab a scone with their teeth, without getting covered in the sticky honey!

MAKES 8 TO 10 LARGE SCONES

240ml (7½fl oz) milk, plus extra for brushing
½ lemon, juiced
100g (3½oz) butter
50g (2oz) brown sugar
400g (14oz) self-raising flour
1 tsp ground cinnamon
1 tsp ground mixed spice
1 tsp baking powder
½ tsp salt
100g (3½oz) rolled oats
2 tbsp honey

1. The first thing you need to do is to sour the milk with the lemon juice. The reason we are souring the milk is to help the chemical reaction with the baking powder that is in the flour, giving you a much better lift and giving you a lighter scone.

2. Preheat the oven to 180°C (350°F).

3. Sift the flour, cinnamon, mixed spice, baking powder and salt into a large bowl.

4. Add three quarters of the rolled oats. Carefully rub in the cold, diced butter.

5. Add the sugar followed by the soured milk to the mixture and knead lightly.

6. Tip out onto a floured surface and roll to a thickness of 4 to 5cm (1 to 1½in).

8. Use a crinkled cutter and cut your scones to the size you require. Place on a non-stick baking sheet. I find that if I bunch them relatively close together I get a better lift. Brush with milk and dust with the remaining oats. Cook for about 12 to 15 minutes until golden brown.

9. Place onto a cooling rack until cold. To finish, drizzle with the honey.

BOW FIDDLE ROCK, PORTKNOCKIE

ST ANDREW'S DAY

St Andrew's Day is celebrated on 30 November. It is a day to commemorate the life and legacy of Scotland's patron saint. It has been celebrated for centuries, with traditions and customs being passed down from generation to generation.

The origins of the celebrations can be traced back over a thousand years, when, according to legend, St Andrew's relics were brought to Scotland. From that time, people began to celebrate St Andrew. By the fourteenth century, St Andrew was established as Scotland's patron saint.

St Andrew's night is celebrated with various activities, such as parades, concerts and fireworks displays. Traditional Scottish food also plays a significant role in the festivities, with dishes such as haggis, neeps and tatties being a popular choice.

Recent years have seen a strong revival of traditional Scottish cuisine, with chefs across the country incorporating local produce and traditional flavours into their menus. Haggis always plays a role in any traditional offering.

St Andrew's night is an important time for Scottish people around the world – an opportunity to celebrate their rich culture, history and heritage. I have been lucky to have supported several St Andrew's dinners. Last year I hosted a very special event at the British High Commission in Barbados. Barbados and Scotland share St Andrew as their patron saint. The year before that I helped with the Feast of the Haggis held at the Chicago Museum. The Feast of the Haggis is an annual fundraising dinner organised by the Chicago Scots who run Caledonia Senior Living and Memory Care on the west side of the city, a Scottish care home which looks after fellow Scots, by birth, by heritage or simply by inclination.

MUSSEL BREE

The best thing about this recipe is that it is very quick and relatively simple to make. Mussels are a brilliant ingredient to cook with and are jam-packed with flavour. I like to add a little bit of whisky to my mussel soup – something peaty and earthy works well with the bold flavour of the mussels. I have also finished this with a little pinch of dried seaweed. It brings a wonderful flavour of the sea to the soup. Dried seaweed can be purchased very easily from speciality food shops and you will also find it online.

1½kg (3lb 4oz) fresh mussels in the shell
200ml (7fl oz) white wine
1 tbsp cooking oil
1 medium onion, finely chopped
1 garlic clove, finely chopped
½ leek, chopped and washed
1 fennel bulb, diced
50ml (2fl oz) whisky, optional
300ml (10fl oz) fish stock
150ml (5fl oz) double cream
Small bunch of flat-leaf parsley, chopped
Pinch of dried seaweed

1. With fresh mussels, it is important to look after them when you buy them. They should be stored in a bucket or tub covered in a sheet or two of wet kitchen paper in the fridge until needed. Do not store mussels in water, as they run out of oxygen very quickly and die.

2. To clean the mussels, wash them under cold running water using a table knife to scrape away any barnacles. You also have to remove the beards that protrude from between the closed shells.

3. If you find any mussels are open, give them a short little tap on the side of the sink; this should encourage them to close. If they do not close, they should be discarded, as they are most likely dead.

4. Place the mussels in a large saucepan, add the white wine and cook for 3 to 4 minutes until they have opened.

5. Place a colander over a large bowl and strain the mussels, reserving the cooking liquor, and pick the mussels from their shells. Discard any that have not opened.

6. Set aside the liquor and the mussels, and throw away the shells.

7. Heat a large saucepan and drizzle with oil.

8. Add the finely chopped onion, garlic, leek and fennel, and cook for 5 to 10 minutes without colouring.

9. Next, add the whisky, fish stock and three-quarters of the mussel meat, and finish with the cream.

10. Bring to a boil and cook for a further 10 minutes until warmed through.

11. Blend with a stick blender, or food processor, until smooth.

12. Finish with the chopped parsley and the remaining mussels, and finally the dried seaweed, if you have some.

GRILLED LANGOUSTINE

WITH SEAWEED BUTTER AND MARIE ROSE DIPPING SAUCE

Langoustine never fails to impress when entertaining: they are a bit of fun, and they look impressive but are remarkably easy to work with. I just love them. When I host events, langoustine are front and centre, and are always the star of the show.

Langoustine thrive in the cold seas and lochs off the shores of Scotland and can easily be bought from a local fishmonger; you can buy them online.

24 langoustine
Salt, 15g (½oz) per litre (quart) of water
150g (5oz) mayonnaise
50g (2oz) tomato ketchup
Few drops of Tabasco sauce
5g (¼oz) smoked paprika
1 lemon, juiced and zested
2 cloves garlic
100g (3½oz) butter
5g (¼oz) dried seaweed flakes
Small bunch of pea shoots

1. The first thing you need to do is to blanch and refresh the langoustine. Bring a large pan of water to a boil and add a generous amount of salt – about 15g (½oz) per litre (quart).

2. Make sure you have a bowl of ice water at the ready to refresh the shellfish once blanched.

3. Plunge the langoustines into the boiling water for 40 seconds and remove and refresh them in the ice-cold water.

4. Once blanched, carefully cut each langoustine in half lengthways. To do this, look for a little cross on the top of the langoustine, and place the point of a large cook's knife into the centre of the cross and push down, cutting through the body and the tail. Remove the knife, give it a clean, and then finish the job by cutting through the head.

5. Once halved, you will notice a brown sack at the head of the langoustine. Carefully remove it. You will also notice the waste tract running through the tail – this will also need to be removed.

6. Repeat with all the langoustine.

7. To make the Marie Rose sauce, mix the mayonnaise with the ketchup, Tabasco sauce and smoked paprika. Finish with a squeeze of lemon juice and put to one side until needed.

8. To make the seaweed butter, crush the garlic, lemon zest and mix with the butter and the seaweed.

9. To cook the langoustine, preheat your grill to medium–high.

10. Lay the langoustine cut-side-up on a large roasting tray and spoon over the seaweed butter. Place under the grill for 3 to 4 minutes, or until the butter is bubbling and the langoustine are golden in colour. Be very careful not to overcook them.

11. Serve immediately, top with some pea shoots and serve with the Marie Rose dipping sauce.

HAGGIS FRITTER

WITH CRISPY SALAD AND WHISKY PEPPERCORN SAUCE

Fritters are very common in certain parts of Scotland and can be found in fish and chip shops (chippies). They are mostly made from potatoes, but some shops and restaurants are making them from haggis nowadays. Super simple to make and, while not the healthiest dish, they make a great alternative to your regular haggis, neeps and tatties on St Andrew's night.

For the haggis fritters

125ml (4fl oz) lager or water
25ml (1fl oz) vinegar
125g (4oz) plain flour, plus extra for dusting
50g (2oz) cornflour
½ tsp salt
1 tsp baking powder
500g (1lb 2oz) haggis, or veggie haggis
Cooking oil for deep frying
Salt, to taste

For the peppercorn whisky sauce

25g (1oz) butter
2 shallots, finely diced
1 tsp cracked black peppercorns
1 tsp pink peppercorns, crushed
1 tsp green peppercorns, crushed
50ml (2fl oz) whisky
85ml (3fl oz) beef stock (a quality cube would work)
200ml (7fl oz) double cream
1 tsp wholegrain mustard
Small bunch of chives, chopped

For the haggis fritters

1. To make the batter, put the lager and vinegar into a large bowl.

2. Next, gradually sieve the plain flour, cornflour, salt and baking powder into the beer and vinegar, whisking as you add. I find if you add the dry ingredients to the liquid, there is less chance of having lumps. The addition of the cornflour will help make the batter super crispy and the addition of the vinegar will keep the batter crispy for longer. The baking powder will add lightness and bubbles to the batter. You might need to add a little more flour to get a nice coating consistency.

3. Once your batter has been prepared, put it to one side until needed.

4. Break the haggis down into 40g (1½oz) balls – you should get 12 balls for 500g (1lb 2oz).

5. Heat the oil in a pan. Press each ball into a flat disk, dip it into your extra flour and then dip it into the batter. Next, carefully lower each disk into the hot oil. Fry for approximately 6 to 8 minutes, or until the batter is crisp and golden, turning the haggis from time to time.

6. Remove from the oil once cooked and drain on some kitchen paper, then season with a touch of salt.

For the peppercorn whisky sauce

1. Add the butter to the pan and heat until it starts to foam gently. Add the finely diced shallots and sweat for 2 to 3 minutes, with as little colour as possible.

2. Once the shallots have gone transparent, add the cracked black peppercorns and crushed pink and green peppercorns. Gently sweat for 30 seconds to 1 minute.

3. Add the whisky and reduce it by half. Next, add the beef stock and again reduce it by half.

4. Pour in the double cream and reduce the heat to a gentle simmer, reducing the sauce by a quarter. The sauce should coat the back of a dessert spoon when ready.

For the salad

1 carrot, cut into matchsticks
1 apple, cut into matchsticks
1 red onion, sliced
50g (2oz) pickled onions
Handful mixed leaves
25ml (1fl oz) good oil
Salt and pepper

5. Whisk in the wholegrain mustard and chopped chives. Check for seasoning, adding a pinch of salt if required.

6. Serve with your haggis fritters.

For the salad

Prepare your carrot, apple and red onion. Mix with the pickled onions and the mixed leaves. Combine with the oil and a little salt and pepper.

GRILLED KING SCALLOPS

WITH FENNEL, CUCUMBER AND CORIANDER, LIME & CARDAMOM BUTTER

Scallops are such an iconic symbol of luxury – especially when served in their shells. Scotland's coastline is the perfect habitat for scallops. Scottish scallops can be found in some of the finest restaurants in the world. I always try and source hand-dived scallops. They are more expensive, but they are sustainable and have very little impact on the environment. If you create this very simple dish, I think it would take centre stage at a very special meal.

- 4 scallops, removed from the shell and cut into 3
- ½ cucumber, cut into spaghetti
- ½ bulb fennel, finely shredded
- 125g (4oz) butter, softened
- 1 lime, juiced and zested
- Small bunch of coriander, chopped
- 8 green cardamom pods, cracked and seeds taken out, pod discarded
- Pinch of dried dulce seaweed, optional
- 1 red chilli, finely diced
- Salt and pepper, to taste

TO NOTE:
You can get scallops in the shell from most good fishmongers. They will be more than happy to shuck them for you. If you fancy giving it a go yourself, it is very easy. You will need a table knife and a spoon for the job.

1. You will notice that the scallop shell has a rounded and a flat shell. Insert your knife into the hinge of the shell and twist it to open it.

2. Run your knife along the inside of the flat shell to separate it from the meat. Once you have the shell completely open, take your spoon and scoop everything out.

3. You now need to remove the white meat and the orange roe from the skirt. I do this by separating them with my fingers.

4. Bin all excess material so you are left with white juicy meat and roe.

5. Give it a quick clean under cold water. Cut each scallop into three slices.

6. Your shells need to be cleaned – you can do this in a dishwasher, or by scrubbing and rinsing them in boiling water.

7. Next, cut the cucumber into spaghetti and shred the fennel bulb.

8. Place the butter into a bowl, and mix in the lime zest and juice, the chopped coriander, cardamom seeds, seaweed, and salt and pepper.

9. Take a piece of parchment paper and roll the butter up so that it resembles a sausage shape. Twist the ends of the paper in opposite directions – doing this will help shape the butter. Pop it in the fridge until firm.

10. Preheat your grill.

11. Place some of the cucumber and fennel in each of the shells, then top with the slices of scallops.

12. Slice the butter into thin disks and place two slices onto the scallops. Sprinkle with diced chilli.

13. Now place under your preheated grill and heat for 4 to 5 minutes or until cooked.

14. Serve immediately.

CHICKEN IN THE HEATHER

This is a perfect dish for a St Andrew's celebration. Getting it in the middle of the table and serving it family style makes for a fun and interactive dinner. Chicken in the heather is a real classic: the heather refers to the heather honey that the chicken is seasoned with. It creates a super tasty glaze.

With this recipe, I am going to be a wee bit less conventional and ask you to cook your chicken upside down – yup, upside down. My thoughts on this are that when the chicken is cooking, gravity draws all the moisture and juices down into the cavity of the bird; we then carve the meat, take the legs off and throw away the carcass, which has all the flavour in it. So, if you cook the bird upside down, the juice and the flavour from the carcass are drawn into the breast meat. Do not worry about the golden crisp skin – we will finish the bird off the right way up to create the lovely golden finish.

---

1 whole chicken (high welfare is much better)
1 onion, roughly chopped
1 carrot, roughly chopped
3 sticks celery, roughly chopped
100g (3½oz) heather honey
2 tsp French mustard
2 tsp curry powder
1 bulb garlic, cut in half through the circumference
2 sprigs of thyme
2 sprigs of rosemary
40cm (16in) butcher's string
25ml (1fl oz) cooking oil
Salt and cracked black pepper

1. Preheat your oven to 200°C (400°F).

2. Whether you choose a standard chicken, free range or organic is a matter of personal choice, but, if possible, go for the best you can afford. Chickens are available in small, medium and large sizes. A small chicken will weigh approximately 1⅕kg (2lb 10oz) and will feed 2 to 3 people. A medium chicken weighs approximately 1¾kg (3lb 14oz) and will feed 3 to 4 people, and a large chicken weighs approximately 2kg (4lb 6oz) and will feed 4 to 6 people.

3. Once all your vegetables are prepared, place them into a deep roasting tray. This will provide a barrier between the hot tray and the chicken; it will also help any juices not to evaporate and the vegetables and juices can then be used to make an incredible gravy.

4. Now to your chicken: you will probably find that your chicken has been trussed with an elastic band. This serves a very important job; it is pulling the bird together; the legs have been pulled in tight against the lower, thinner part of the breast. Doing this helps the bird cook more evenly, as the legs protect the breast meat.

5. You will need to remove the band for now. Have a look inside the bird's cavity and you might find a little bag of innards – if so, open it up and remove the liver and put to one side. Pop everything else on the tray with

recipe continues on the next page

the chopped vegetables. You can use the liver separately in another dish, but it is not great to make a sauce.

6. In a small bowl, mix your honey with the mustard and the curry powder.

7. You are now ready to prepare the chicken for the oven. With a generous pinch of salt, season the inside of the cavity and the outside of the bird. Stuff the cavity with half the bulb of garlic and the herbs; take some oil and rub it into the chicken skin.

8. Take your honey mixture and massage it into the skin of the chicken, making sure you cover the entire bird.

9. Next, replace the elastic band around the chicken. If you don't have one, use some string.

10. Place the bird on the tray, breast side down, and pop it into the oven: the length of time is dependent on the weight of the bird – the guide is 40 minutes per 1kg (2lb 3oz) plus 20 minutes.

11. Calculate your total time in the oven and cook the chicken upside down for three-quarters of the time, then carefully turn it right side up and finish the cooking.

12. Baste the bird frequently as it roasts.

13. How do you know if the bird is cooked, as the chicken must be thoroughly cooked before serving, without any pink meat? Pierce the thickest part of the thigh with a skewer and let the juices run out. If they are clear, then it's cooked, but if they still look pink, return it to the oven for 15 minutes, then test again. If you have a meat thermometer, push the probe into the thickest part of the thigh. The temperature should be 75°C (167°F) before serving.

14. The next stage is vital: rest the bird before carving. This should be done for at least 30 minutes. Resting allows the meat to settle and relax, which helps to keep it moist.

15. To carve the bird, I would remove the legs by popping them off their ball and socket joint at the pelvic bone. Each leg can be cut into two joints, the thigh and the drumstick, giving four pieces of brown meat.

16. Next, take a carving knife and cut the breast meat into thin slices until you reach the carcass; do this on both sides until you have recovered all the meat.

17. Serve with vegetables and potatoes of your choice.

18. Make sure you keep the remaining carcass, as it makes the most amazing roast gravy. You can adapt the recipe on page 152 to make a chicken gravy.

PAN-SEARED PLAICE

WITH CELERIAC, SPRING ONION, PEAR AND HOLLANDAISE SAUCE

Cooking fish on the bone is becoming a lost art in Scotland, but there are real benefits to preparing fish in this way. It is much quicker, as the heat travels through the bone and helps the fish cook in the middle; it also retains more moisture. Plaice is a very under-used fish – we always use plaice to teach our students how to fillet fish. It is brilliant – full of flavour, with a fantastic texture. I am not sure why we don't see it more often.

For the plaice

2 whole plaice (sole will work just as well)
½ head celeriac, diced
50g (2oz) flour, seasoned
25g (1oz) butter
1 lemon, juiced
12 spring onions
1 pear
Salad cress, to finish
Cooking oil

For the hollandaise sauce

150g (5oz) butter
25ml (1fl oz) white wine vinegar
25ml (1fl oz) water
½ shallot, finely diced
3 whole black peppercorns
½ lemon, juiced
4 egg yolks
Salt

For the plaice

1. The first task is to prepare the fish. This is not as hard as it looks. Take your fish and, with a pair of scissors, trim off the fins that run along each side. Next, cut off the head and then cut 3cm (1in) slices through the bone all the way down. You should get 4 to 6 slices per fish.

2. Don't worry about the skin and any loose bones, as these are easily removed once the fish is cooked.

3. Cut the celeriac into 1cm (⅓in) dice and pan-fry with oil until crisp and soft in the centre.

4. Place a large frying pan onto the stove and heat it. Whilst the pan is heating, coat each fillet in seasoned flour.

5. Place the fish into the pan, cut side first. Cook until golden brown and finish with a knob of butter and a good squeeze of lemon juice.

6. Meantime, trim the spring onions and cook in a hot pan.

7. Cut the fresh pear into matchsticks.

8. Take the fish from the pan and carefully remove the skin and any loose bones.

9. To serve, place the cooked fillets onto the plate and top with the spring onion, celeriac and pear. Garnish with the salad cress.

recipe continues on the next page

For the hollandaise sauce

1. To start, clarify the butter by placing it into a heavy-based pan and gently heating it – but without boiling it. You will notice the butter separates (the milky whey sinks to the bottom and the clear fat lies on top). Try not to disturb the pan too much by shaking or stirring; remove from the heat and allow to settle for 2 to 3 minutes.

2. Meanwhile, place the vinegar, water, diced shallot, peppercorns and lemon juice into a separate pan and bring to a boil, reducing by a quarter.

3. Once the butter has settled, take a ladle and start to carefully lift off the clarified butter and put into a microwave-safe pouring jug. Again, try not to disturb the whey at the bottom of the pan.

4. Pass the water and vinegar reduction through a fine sieve to remove the peppercorns and shallots.

5. Place the egg yolks into a steel bowl and slowly add the reduction to the egg yolks.

6. Gradually add the melted butter. The mixture should start to thicken. Slowly drizzle in the clarified butter until all the butter is used. If the sauce is too thick, add a teaspoon of water to thin it down.

7. Taste and season with salt if required. Serve while the sauce is still warm.

ST ANDREW'S VEGGIE PIE

This is a brilliant alternative to the traditional steak pie. The addition of the veggie haggis really makes it special. I am a big fan of veggie haggis – it has all the big flavours, and most of the same ingredients as regular haggis, it makes a fantastic dish in its own right. Its history is well documented. It was invented by John MacSween in 1984, especially for the opening of the Scottish Poetry Library in Edinburgh. The meat-free haggis, served to all the guests, was met with wide acclaim and astonishment.

MacSween's veggie haggis has become a classic, enjoyed by veggies, vegans and carnivores alike. It is a fantastic alternative for me when I am doing events in the US, as meat-based Scottish haggis is banned because it contains lung.

See page 162 for the hot-water pastry recipe.

For the filling

150g (5oz) carrots, diced
150g (5oz) leeks, diced
150g (5oz) parsnips, diced
150g (5oz) butternut squash, diced
2 onions, chopped
1 tbsp good oil
100ml (3½fl oz) beer
25g (1oz) plain flour
500g (1lb 2oz) veggie haggis
1 tbsp parsley, chopped
1 tbsp thyme, chopped
Salt and ground black pepper
300ml (10fl oz) vegetable stock (a quality cube will work for this)
50ml (2fl oz) dark soy sauce
1 egg, beaten, for the glaze

NOTE:
I would make the filling first, as the pastry works best when rolled whilst it is still hot.

For the filling

1. The first task is to wash, peel and chop your vegetables.

2. Once you have done that, heat the oil in a large heavy-bottomed pan and fry the vegetables until they take on a little bit of colour.

3. Next, add the beer and then dust with the flour. Keep stirring until the flour has completely mixed with the vegetables and beer, without any lumps.

4. Next, mix in the veggie haggis.

5. Add the herbs, salt and ground black pepper, then the stock. Bring to a boil.

6. Add a little of your soy sauce to darken the gravy.

7. Cook slowly on the stove until the vegetables are tender. Put to one side.

For the pie

1. Preheat the oven to 200°C (400°F).

2. Roll out half of your pastry and line a 20cm (8in) pastry ring or pie dish.

3. Next, fill with your cooled filling, then roll out the other half of the pastry and top the pie.

4. Brush with beaten egg and decorate, if you wish, using the pastry trimmings. I have used a thistle cutter to make a decorative top.

5. Bake in the oven for 20 minutes at 200°C (400°F), then turn the oven down to 160°C (325°F) for 30 minutes.

6. Allow the pie to settle for 20 minutes before cutting.

SPICED RIBEYE STEAK

WITH BUTTER BEAN AND KALE STEW

This is a lovely dish, using ribeye steak. I think, out of all the prime cuts, this is the best. I love the level of fat that is in the steak; it adds so much to the flavour and the texture of the meat, and it also helps it to retain moisture. If you want the very best meat available, look out for 'Scotch beef' on the label. This means that the beef is from specific animals that are sourced from selected Scottish farms, adopting best practice, which includes animal welfare and natural production methods.

It is best to start this recipe the night before as you will need to soak the butterbeans and marinate the steak

For the steak
½ tsp coriander seeds
½ tsp cumin seeds
3 sprigs of rosemary
½ tsp Cajun seasoning
25ml (1fl oz) cooking oil
4x 200g (7oz) ribeye steak

For the stew
200g (7oz) dried butter beans, soaked overnight
2 sprigs of rosemary
2 sprigs of thyme
3 garlic clove, crushed
1 red onion, chopped
3 tomatoes, chopped
1 x 400g (14oz) tin chopped tomatoes
100ml (3½fl oz) red wine
1 tsp Cajun seasoning
1 tbsp tomato purée
1 tbsp red wine vinegar
Small bunch of kale, shredded
1 tbsp fresh basil, chopped
1 tbsp fresh parsley, chopped

For the steak

1. For this recipe, I would marinate the meat overnight. Start by dry-roasting the coriander and cumin seeds, then crush them in a grinder or a pestle and mortar.

2. Chop the rosemary and mix the toasted spice with the Cajun seasoning, then add the oil.

3. Pop the steaks in a bag and add the marinade. Massage it into the meat and store it in the fridge until the next day.

For the stew

1. Place the soaked beans in a medium pot covered with cold water, then add the rosemary, thyme and one clove of garlic.

2. Slowly bring to a boil and cook until softened.

3. Heat a little oil in a saucepan over a medium heat.

4. Add the chopped red onion and the rest of the garlic and fry for 3 to 4 minutes until they are golden brown all over. Be careful not to burn the garlic.

5. Add the remaining stew ingredients, except for the fresh herbs and the kale.

6. Bring to a boil, then simmer for 10 to 12 minutes.

7. Add the herbs and the kale and stir well.

8. Pop a skillet or a pan onto the stove, making sure the pan is hot. Add your steaks and sear on both sides quickly.

9. Allow the steak to rest before serving it with your stew.

MARY, QUEEN OF SCOTS TARTLETS

Mary, Queen of Scots is perhaps the most iconic monarch in Scottish history, her story deeply resonates with people across the world. Despite dying centuries ago, she remains a cultural icon. Kids today still recite the poem recounting her demise. My son, Cameron, who is working on his PhD in history, recently made a contribution to a Mary, Queen of Scots exhibition at the Hunterian Museum, focusing on her coins.

As for the origins of this tart, I guess it might be that Mary, Queen of Scots was said to be a fan of marmalade, and there is citrus peel in the recipe. I like to think that one of her royal chefs created it for her. Whatever the origins, this is a wonderful little recipe that's worth giving a try.

MAKES 12 TARTLETS

For the pastry
- 125g (4oz) butter
- 200g (8oz) plain flour
- Pinch of salt
- 1 egg
- 50g (2oz) caster sugar

For the filling
- 100g (3½oz) butter
- 100g (3½oz) caster sugar
- 2 eggs
- Few drops of vanilla extract
- 50g (2oz) plain flour
- 200g (7oz) sultanas
- 150g (5oz) chopped mixed candied peel

For the pastry

1. Rub the butter, flour and the salt together until you have a breadcrumb texture. Make sure that you can still see some small lumps of butter at the end of the rubbing-in process.

2. Crack the egg into a bowl and then add the sugar and lightly mix.

3. Add the egg and sugar mix to the flour and butter, then using the palm of your hand bring this mixture together to form a dough. Please make sure you don't overwork the dough at this stage.

4. Next, flatten out the pastry to form a disk about 3cm (1in) thick.

5. Cling film the pastry and place it into the fridge to rest.

For the filling

1. Cream the butter and the sugar together until they are light and fluffy.

2. Beat your eggs together with the vanilla extract, then gradually add them to the butter and sugar mix, whisking the whole time.

3. Once all the eggs are added, fold in the flour, sultanas and mixed peel.

To assemble

1. Roll out your pastry and cut 12 circles big enough to fill your pastry rings.

2. Carefully line the rings, then fill the pastry with the filling.

3. Preheat the oven to 160°C (325°F).

4. Bake your tartlets for 25 to 30 minutes until golden brown.

5. Allow to stand for 10 minutes before removing from the rings.

WINTER PLUM, HAZELNUT & CHOCOLATE CAKE

This recipe for a delicious plum and hazelnut cake is a firm favourite with the family and they always ask for it. This is a beautiful combination of winter plums, nuts and chocolate. It can also be made into individual cakes or even cupcakes. This is perfect for celebrating St Andrew's Day with friends and family.

500g (1lb 2oz) plums

170g (6oz) butter, plus extra for greasing

170g (6oz) light-brown sugar

170g (6oz) self-raising flour

170g (6oz) ground hazelnuts

3 eggs

1 tsp baking powder

100g (3½oz) dark chocolate, chopped

2 tbsp chopped hazelnuts

50g (2oz) plum jam

1. The first job is to butter and line the base of a round 20cm (8in) spring-form cake tin with parchment paper.

2. Halve and stone four plums, setting them aside for later. Roughly chop the remaining plums and set them aside as well.

3. In a large bowl, beat together the butter, sugar, self-raising flour, ground hazelnuts, eggs and baking powder with an electric hand or stand mixer until smooth and light.

4. Preheat the oven to 160°C (325°F).

5. Stir in the chopped plums and chopped dark chocolate, then pour the mixture into the prepared cake tin and smooth the top.

6. Arrange the halved plums over the top of the mixture and press them down lightly.

7. Scatter the chopped hazelnuts over the top.

8. Bake for 40 to 50 minutes until the top is golden and the cake feels firm to the touch. Cool the cake in the tin for 10 minutes, then turn it out onto a wire rack to cool completely.

9. Finally, heat the plum jam and brush it over the top of the cake before serving.

BUACHAILLE ETIVE MÒR, GLEN ETIVE

CHRISTMAS

CHRISTMAS

Celebrating Christmas in Scotland is a fairly new tradition. It was always Hogmanay that was favoured as the celebration of choice. The reason for this was that Christmas was actually banned in Scotland for 400 years. Christmas Day was a normal working day for most people up to the 1950s. So, if there is a specifically 'Scottish' aspect to Christmas, it is that it was not celebrated!

I would say my generation was one of the first to have a big Christmas. It wasn't until recently that I learned from my mum how different her Christmas was to the one I grew up with.

The 'traditional' celebrations of the festive season that we know of today originated in the nineteenth century. Prince Albert, Queen Victoria's husband, had a lot to do with that, as he brought Germanic traditions to Britain. England adopted Christmas trees, decorations, Saint Nicholas, presents, stockings at the end of the bed and Christmas carols, while Scotland was to follow – but much later.

Charles Dickens is also credited with saving Christmas and reigniting what is now one of the biggest celebrations in the Western world. When Dickens wrote *A Christmas Carol* in 1842, the whole idea of Christmas was nearly dead in middle-class and affluent England and non-existent in Scotland. Christmas was only celebrated by the rural and the poor, but the popularity of the book sparked a tremendous new interest that we still have today.

We also have Queen Victoria and Prince Albert to thank for the tradition of eating turkey at Christmas. The tradition in the royal household was to always eat swan, but they made the switch in the 1850s. Regular households always went for goose.

Fast-forward to the present day and the Scots now fully embrace Christmas and its customs. We follow the same food traditions as the rest of the UK, though we probably drink more whisky and eat more smoked salmon, but that is it. Some people hold some ancient traditions, like keeping a fire burning through Christmas to ward away evil spirits. Mistletoe hung from the ceiling or in doorways is also said to keep evil spirits out and bring in good fortune. I am not superstitious, but this is one tradition I have in my home.

Christmas is a very special time for most families and food is always at the heart of it.

CARNEGIE BRIE & CRANBERRY BITES

This is a fun festive canapé that can be done in advance and heated when needed. I think they look very festive. Once you have mastered the little baskets, you can add all sorts of different fillings to them. I have used a wonderful cheese called Carnegie Brie. This is a delicious, rich and creamy cheese made in Tain in the Scottish Highlands.

MAKES 6 TO 8 PORTIONS

3 sheets filo pastry
25g (1oz) butter, melted
50g (2oz) Carnegie Brie
25g (1oz) cranberry sauce
Pinch of chives, chopped

1. The first job is to make the little filo baskets. This is very easy, and if you have a small muffin tin it will be even easier.

2. Take the 3 sheets of filo pastry and cut them in half, then half again, and keep cutting until you get a bundle of squares of pastry about 6cm (2½in) wide.

3. Each basket will use 3 squares of pastry. Take a square and brush with the melted butter. Next, add another square on top, but this time change the angle slightly. Lastly, add the third square on top of that. If you have got your angles right, it should look like a star.

4. Push your star of pastry into the muffin tin.

5. Repeat until all the pastry has been used up.

6. Preheat your oven to 180°C (350°F).

7. Bake in the oven for 4 to 6 minutes until golden brown.

8. Next, cut the Brie into ½cm (¼in) pieces.

9. Fill each of your cooked baskets with the Brie and top with a little cranberry sauce.

10. Pop back into the oven for 3 to 4 minutes or until the Brie starts to melt.

11. Top with some chopped chives.

CRANBERRY & SAGE SAUSAGE ROLLS

This is a delicious and festive recipe to serve at your Christmas party. These tasty treats combine the rich, savoury flavour of pork sausage with the tart sweetness of fresh cranberries, all wrapped up in a flaky puff pastry crust. Perfect for snacking or as a main dish, these sausage rolls are sure to be a hit with your family. Using the same method, you can change the flavours to anything you like – all that's stopping you is your imagination.

MAKES 4 TO 6 PORTIONS

2 shallots, chopped
6 sage leaves, shredded
400g (14oz) sausage meat
100g (3½oz) dried cranberries
1 egg yolk
375g (13oz) pre-rolled puff pastry
25ml (1fl oz) cooking oil
Pinch of poppy seeds, optional
Mixed leaves, optional

1. Add a little oil to a pan and add the chopped shallots. Cook them slowly and once translucent add the shredded sage leaves and cook for another 60 seconds. Remove from the heat.

2. Meanwhile, pop the sausage meat into a bowl with the dried cranberries. Once the shallot mix has cooled, add to the sausage meat and cranberries and mix well.

3. Next, break the egg and separate the yolk from the white.

4. You are on to the fun part now! Remove the pastry from the packaging and carefully roll it out, using the baking paper to assist.

5. Cut three sections of pastry about 10cm (4in) long from the roll.

6. Lay out the pastry, weigh roughly 3x 150g (5oz) of your sausage mix and shape it into a long cylinder, then place it lengthwise at the closest edge of the pastry.

7. Brush the exposed part of the pastry with the egg yolk, then turn the pastry over the sausage meat and roll up, making sure it is tight. Repeat for the other sheets of pastry.

8. Next, chill and set your sausage rolls for about an hour.

9. Remove from the fridge and brush your sausage rolls with the egg yolk.

10. Using a sharp knife, score the top of your rolls and sprinkle with poppy seeds, if you are using them.

11. Put them back in the fridge.

12. To cook, bake in a preheated oven (200°C/400°F) for 15 to 20 minutes until golden brown.

13. Once cold, cut the logs into bite-sized pieces.

14. Serve with mixed leaves.

PANKO & SCOTTISH CHEDDAR BRUSSELS SPROUTS

I have spent my whole career moaning about Brussels sprouts. As a young chef, I spent most of the festive season preparing Brussels sprouts; I watched the customers' food going out with three or four sprouts on each plate and then at the end of the meal I watched the plates come back in with the same three or four sprouts on them. I didn't see the point. Over the years, I have endeavoured to love them, and the more I work with them and treat them with care, I am finding more ways to make them delicious.

MAKES 6 TO 8 PORTIONS

500g (1lb 2oz) Brussels sprouts
85g (3oz) panko crumbs
50g (2oz) flour seasoned
Pinch of chilli powder
1 egg
Splash of milk
Cooking oil for baking
50g (2oz) Scottish hard Cheddar cheese, to serve
Salt and pepper

1. Your first job is to prepare and cook your sprouts. To do this, cut the root end off the sprouts and then cut a small cross into each at the cut end. This little cut helps cook the sprouts through the middle more evenly.

2. Cook in boiling salted water for about 3 to 4 minutes. You will notice that the sprouts turn bright green; once this happens, remove them immediately and cool them in cold water.

3. Once cooled, dry off on a little kitchen paper.

4. Preheat the oven to 200°C (400°F).

5. The next task is to coat the sprouts in panko crumbs. To do this you will need what is called a pané system. This consists of three trays: one with seasoned flour (I added a pinch of chilli to my flour to add a little heat), one with an egg and a little milk, and a third with breadcrumbs.

6. In this order, roll the sprouts in the flour and chilli, next the egg and milk mixture, and lastly the panko crumbs.

7. Place the coated sprouts onto a tray and coat them with a little oil.

8. Bake for about 20 minutes, making sure you shoogle the tray now and again.

9. Remove from the tray.

10. Using a potato peeler, peel shreds from a piece of Scottish Cheddar cheese, top the sprouts and serve.

PARSNIP & SMOKED CHEDDAR SOUP

This is a hearty soup. The addition of a little spice and the smoked cheese makes this very special. It is just perfect for cold winter nights or as a light meal when you're still full on Boxing Day.

MAKES 4 TO 6 PORTIONS

250g (9oz) onions, chopped

1kg (2lb 3oz) parsnips, peeled and roughly chopped

50g (2oz) butter

1 tsp chilli powder

2 litre (2 quarts) vegetable stock (a stock cube would work for this)

100ml (3½fl oz) double cream

100g (3½oz) smoked Cheddar cheese, grated

½ tsp cayenne pepper

1. Peel and chop your onion and parsnips into even sizes.

2. Melt the butter in a saucepan and then add the roughly chopped onions.

3. Cook without colouring. Once soft and clear, add in the parsnips and the chilli powder.

4. Cover with stock and simmer until the parsnips are soft. This should take about 20 to 25 minutes.

5. Remove the pot from the heat, then blitz until smooth with a hand blender. Note: make sure the parsnips are soft before blitzing otherwise you can end up with stringy bits through the soup.

6. Add half of the double cream and all the cheese.

7. Put the soup back onto the heat, double check the seasoning, and heat until the cheese has melted through the soup.

8. Spoon a swirl of cream over the top of each bowl and a sprinkle of cayenne pepper.

THE BEST CHRISTMAS TURKEY

Turkey has a long association with Christmas. It has been on the tables of the well-heeled for over 500 years; Henry VIII was the first king documented to have eaten it at Christmas.

During Victorian times, it became really popular due to the fact that Queen Victoria loved Christmas – she popularised many of the traditions we adhere to today.

Turkey also got a huge lift in popularity when it made an appearance in the Charles Dickens novel *A Christmas Carol* – Ebenezer Scrooge presents the Cratchit family with a huge turkey on Christmas day. However, it was not until after the Second World War, when farming methods changed and made it less expensive for the average family, that it became the iconic must-have roast on the table at Christmas.

As most people only cook one turkey a year, it can sometimes be a daunting task. Everyone is seeking advice on their turkeys, from what size they need to how long to cook it. I was once part of a campaign to save the equivalent of 100,000 turkeys from going in the bin due to people overcooking or buying a bird that is far too big for their needs. By following some basic principles, I can guarantee a perfectly moist, tender turkey, which should relieve some of the pressure on the big day.

Use the best produce you can afford, so don't scrimp on the turkey. It's going to be the star of any Christmas meal. I would rather have less of something good, than more of something poor.

I always buy as locally as possible, so I look for the country of origin, and high-welfare turkeys taste better. I prefer free-range, as it really makes a difference.

Have a look inside the cavity and the neck end of the bird, and check for a bag of innards. Take them out and put them to one side. This bag will be used in the bottom of your tray when roasting. The bits and bobs will add loads of flavour to the gravy.

Brining turkey has become very popular in recent years. If you have the time and a bucket big enough, it helps keep the moisture and adds extra crispiness to the skin, but it can make your gravy a little salty. The brine is made by adding around 50g (2oz) of salt to every litre (quart) of water; you can use other liquids, such as beer, wine or fruit juice. I would also suggest that you use a good quality salt. I find table salt far too harsh. You can also add herbs and spices to this brine solution. I would suggest that you should brine a turkey for no more than 1 hour per 500g (1lb 2oz), so a 4kg (9lb) bird would take 8 hours. Once you have brined the bird, rinse it off in cold water and pat dry, then pop it in the fridge to air dry.

Do not stuff the turkey with stuffing! I know that sounds a bit strange but due to the shape of the cavity, the stuffing may not cook evenly and, except for the small amount that sticks out of the end, it does not develop a crust. More importantly, by the time the centre of the stuffing is cooked to a safe temperature, the breast meat on the turkey will be overcooked and dry. Make your stuffing separately. I roll it up tightly in foil and bake it in the oven, allow it to cool and slice (see the recipe on the next page).

Season the turkey thoroughly. You need to be generous with the salt and pepper – a pinch of salt is not going to season a 7½kg (16lb 8oz) bird! And always season inside the cavity – I avoid seasoning the skin, as it won't absorb salt and just leaves a crust; what I do is mix the salt and pepper into room temperature butter and push it between the skin and the flesh, which helps keep the meat moist and well-seasoned.

Basting is the real key to getting a lovely moist turkey. Fat helps protect the meat and stops it from drying out in the cooking process.

Trussing or tying the turkey is important because it does two things: one, it plumps the breasts for carving, and two, it keeps the legs close to the rest of the carcass, which stops the turkey from drying out. The legs protect the narrow part of the breast and help the bird cook evenly.

Bring your turkey out of the fridge for one hour before roasting to take the chill off. Then take two carrots, two sticks of celery and an onion and cut them into large chunks and place them on the bottom of a deep roasting pan. I put the turkey breast side down on top of the vegetables. The theory behind cooking it upside down is that all the juices are pulled into the turkey breast by gravity and not into the carcass that ends up in the bin.

For the last 40 minutes, turn the turkey the correct way up to finish the cooking and to achieve a golden brown colour. Add about a half-inch of water to the roasting pan and place it in the preheated oven. This will help keep the oven moist and capture the juices that escape the turkey. This liquid can be used to baste the turkey while it cooks, along with all the juices and fats that are going to be released and eventually turned into golden-rich gravy.

This little chart below will give you an idea of what size turkey to purchase. It is not an exact science, and some people eat more than others, but also leftover turkey can be turned into loads of amazing dishes.

KG	LB	SERVES
2½–3	5½lb–6lb 10oz	4–6
3½–4	7lb 12oz–9lb	7–9
4½–5	9lb 15oz–11lb	9–10
5½–6	12lb–13lb 4oz	10–12
6½–7	14lb 5oz–15lb 7oz	12–14
7½–8	16lb 8oz–17lb 10oz	15–17
8+	18lb +	18+

As a guide, if the bird is under 4kg (9lb) I cook it for 20 minutes per kg and then I add 70 minutes on to that time. If the bird is over 4kg (9lb) I still cook it for 20 minutes per kg, but I add 90 minutes on to that time. My timings are for a preheated fan-assisted oven at 190°C (375°F).

You must let the turkey rest for at least 1 hour. When you remove it from the oven, turn the turkey upside down and rest it on its breasts. Cover it very loosely with foil and go about getting everything else ready. It won't get cold; a covered turkey will stay hot for well over an hour.

Letting it rest not only gives you time to finish the gravy, and the rest of the meal, but also allows the juices in the turkey to redistribute, which is the secret to the moist, tender meat. You can adapt the recipe on page 152 to make a turkey gravy.

PORK, APPLE & SAGE STUFFING

Traditionally, it is expected that you stuff the turkey – hence the name. But I always make the stuffing separately. It is easier to cook that way; it is also easier to portion and can be done in advance. Stuffing is a real favourite in my house. It's the one thing that everyone sneaks into the kitchen to grab an early taste of.

MAKES 4 TO 6 PORTIONS

Small red onion, peeled and finely diced

1 stick celery, peeled and chopped into fine dice

1 green apple, peeled and finely diced

Small bunch of flat-leaf parsley, shredded

1 egg

400g (14oz) pork sausage meat

85g (3oz) fresh breadcrumbs

Cracked black pepper

1 tsp dried sage

Splash of cooking oil

1. Prepare and chop all your ingredients.

2. Gently fry off the chopped onion and celery in a little oil in a frying pan.

3. Once cooked, allow to cool.

4. In a bowl, combine the diced apple, shredded parsley, egg, the celery and onion mix, the sausage meat, and mix well.

5. Lastly, add the fresh breadcrumbs, a few turns of black pepper and sage. Mix this all together.

6. Split the mix into two equal balls. Take two sheets of tin foil and place them onto the work surface.

7. Add a ball to the edge of each sheet and shape each ball into a long sausage shape.

8. Carefully roll the sausage-shaped stuffing up in the foil.

9. Once you have rolled them up, twist the ends of the foil in opposite directions to create a tight cylinder.

10. To cook, place in a preheated oven at 180°C (350°F) and bake for 20 to 25 minutes or until the core temperature reaches 75°C (167°F).

11. Allow to cool and remove the foil before slicing.

HONEY ROAST PARSNIPS

You simply cannot have a Christmas dinner without the inclusion of parsnips. They have a very distinct flavour and work well in many recipes, as they can be cooked in lots of different ways. This recipe is very traditional, with one exception being the addition of Worcestershire sauce. This adds a little bit of spice and helps to balance out the sweetness of the honey and the parsnips.

MAKES 4 TO 6 PORTIONS

1kg (2lb 3oz) parsnips
50g (2oz) butter
50g (2oz) honey
1 tsp Worcestershire sauce
Small bunch of chives, chopped
25ml (1fl oz) cooking oil
Salt and pepper

1. Preheat the oven to 180°C (350°F).

2. Peel, then cut the top and bottom off the parsnips.

3. Cut into quarters lengthwise, then carefully cut the hard woody core bit from the middle of each quarter.

4. Tip into a large tray, drizzle with oil, season with salt and ground black pepper, toss to coat in the oil, then arrange in a single layer on the tray.

5. Place into the hot oven and cook for 20 to 25 minutes until the parsnips are golden and start to soften.

6. Meanwhile, in a small pan melt the butter with the honey and the Worcestershire sauce.

7. Remove the tray from the oven and drizzle with the butter mix, then toss everything together and roast for a further 10 minutes, or until beautifully golden.

8. Remove from the oven and finish with the chopped chives.

BRUSSELS SPROUTS

WITH CRISPY BACON

Christmas can't be Christmas without Brussels sprouts on the table. It has taken me a long time to appreciate them. My family loves them, especially my younger kids. They are always the first to disappear with a bowlful. The addition of bacon and Worcestershire sauce makes this a brilliant way to add a bit of luxury to the humble sprout.

300g (11oz) Brussels sprouts
100g (3½oz) streaky bacon, diced
25g (1oz) butter
1 tsp Worcestershire sauce
Good oil
Salt and pepper

1. The first task is to prepare the sprouts. Slice the bottom off each sprout and cut a cross into the exposed base.

2. Remove any damaged outer leaves.

3. In a pan of boiling salted water, cook the sprouts for about 2 minutes, then refresh in cold water.

4. Once cool, cut them in half.

5. Meanwhile, dice the bacon.

6. In a large frying pan, heat a teaspoon of oil.

7. When hot, add the bacon and cook over a high heat for 3 to 4 minutes, or until the bacon is golden and crispy.

8. Drain in a colander, reserving the fat.

9. Wipe out the pan and add in one teaspoon of the reserved fat and the butter.

10. When the butter foams, add the sprouts and sauté for 2 to 3 minutes, then return the bacon to the pan.

11. Cook together until thoroughly hot. Finish with a dash of Worcestershire sauce.

12. Double check seasoning and serve.

GOOSE-FAT ROAST POTATOES

You cannot have a Christmas dinner without goose-fat roasted potatoes. I add semolina to create a bit more of a crunch. I would go as far as saying that if you have good gravy and a plate of goose-fat roast potatoes you don't need much else on your plate. With this recipe, I have brined the potatoes – brining will add a bit of time to the recipe, but I think it is worth it. It will add loads of flavour and crispness to the potatoes.

MAKES 6 TO 8 PORTIONS

2kg (4lb 6oz) potatoes (Maris Piper, Red Rooster)
3 sprigs of rosemary
4 cloves garlic
25g (1oz) black peppercorns
150g (5oz) goose or duck fat
3 sprigs of thyme
25g (1oz) coarse salt
100g (3½oz) semolina

1. Peel and wash the potatoes and cut them into even sizes.

2. Place the potatoes, rosemary, garlic and peppercorns into a large saucepan.

3. Cover with water and add salt.

4. Bring to a boil over a high heat.

5. Reduce heat to medium and simmer for 5 minutes.

6. Turn off the heat. Let the potatoes stand in the brine for at least 5 to 6 hours.

7. Preheat the oven to 200°C (400°F).

8. Drain the potatoes and dry them with some kitchen paper.

9. Put them in a bowl with the goose or duck fat, thyme, salt and semolina, and give it a good mix.

10. Place onto a large tray, making sure that you give each potato some room.

11. Place into the oven. Every now and then, give the tray a shoogle.

12. Cook until golden crispy. They should all have a fluffy, soft centre. The time it takes to achieve this depends on the size of your potatoes.

TURKEY WELLINGTON

This recipe is perfect if you want to have turkey on Christmas day but want something a little different. Do not be frightened to give this a go; it is much easier than you think. The best bit about this recipe is that it can be done a day or two in advance, giving you more time on the big day to do other things.

MAKES 4 TO 6 PORTIONS

2 banana shallots, chopped
Small bunch of thyme
Small bunch of sage, shredded
2 garlic cloves
25g (1oz) butter
600g (1lb 5oz) pork sausage meat
50g (2oz) panko breadcrumbs
2 eggs, plus 1 extra for glazing at the end
4x 150g (5oz) turkey escallops
100g (3½oz) Parma ham
500g (1lb 2oz) puff pastry
50g (2oz) dried cranberries
25g (1oz) good oil
Salt and pepper

1. Your first task is to make the stuffing. Add a little oil to a medium-hot pan and cook the shallots until they have softened.

2. Add the thyme leaves, the sage and the garlic.

3. Remove from the heat and add the butter. Mix until melted, then cool.

4. Place your sausage meat into a mixing bowl, add the breadcrumbs, cranberries, an egg and the cold shallot mixture. Mix well and season with salt and pepper.

5. Next, lay two or three sheets of cling film onto the worktop and place your four escallops of turkey onto the sheets, with a little overlap so that you have a continuous line of turkey.

6. Season the turkey with a little salt and pepper, and spread the stuffing mix onto the turkey escallops.

7. Using the cling film, roll the turkey escallop and stuffing up into a spiral shape. Tighten into a cylinder by twisting the ends of the film in opposite directions. Place in the fridge to set.

8. Next, lay a large sheet of tin foil onto your surface. Place your Parma ham onto the foil, the same width as the turkey roll.

9. Remove your turkey from the cling film and place it onto the ham. Roll the ham around the turkey and then rewrap.

10. Meanwhile, roll the puff pastry large enough to wrap around the parcel.

11. Remove the turkey roll from the tin foil and wrap in the puff pastry.

12. Take your pastry trimmings and roll into a flat sheet; using a lattice pastry cutter, cut the pastry into a lattice (these cutters can be picked up very easily in cookshops or online).

13. Transfer to a baking sheet and brush the pastry with a beaten egg yolk.

14. Carefully drape the lattice

pastry on top of the wellington and then brush again with egg yolk.

15. Preheat your oven to 200°C (400°F).

16. Cook the wellington in the oven for 30 to 40 minutes. You need the oven to be very hot to get the pastry cooked – having a digital temperature probe helps with this, as you would need to take this to a core temperature of 75°C (165°F).

17. Once cooked, allow to rest. Slice and serve with turkey gravy. You can adapt the recipe on page 152 to make a turkey gravy.

CHRISTMAS PUDDING
WITH BRANDY SAUCE

I take pride in writing recipes that are practical, use minimal ingredients and are quick to make. However, I must warn you that this particular recipe does not fit that bill. Nevertheless, I wholeheartedly believe that it is worth trying at least once in your life.

In my opinion, Christmas pudding is an essential part of any festive feast. It can be used in a multitude of other dishes as well, such as soufflés, chocolate fondant, and bread and butter puddings. By adding this pudding to classic recipes, it can instantly transform them into a festive favourite. The options are endless!

Every year, my college makes a large batch of Christmas pudding in the middle of November, which signals the start of the festive season for me. The smell of this dessert is the very essence of Christmas, and it sustains us through the entire month of December.

Please feel free to customise this recipe based on your favourite ingredients or add your own twist to make it a family tradition.

recipe starts on the next page

MAKES 8 TO 10 PORTIONS

For the pudding

450g (1lb) dried mixed fruit (sultanas, raisins and currants)
100g (3½oz) dried apricots, sliced
100g (3½oz) chopped candied peel
2 oranges, juiced and zested
100g (3½oz) muscovado sugar
150ml (5fl oz) whisky
100g (3½oz) sliced almonds
100g (3½oz) chopped walnuts
100g (3½oz) ground almonds
150g (5oz) fresh white breadcrumbs
50g (1oz) self-raising flour
200g (7oz) suet (veggie suet also works)
1 tsp ground cinnamon
2 tsp mixed spice
100g (3½oz) chopped glacé cherries
4 eggs, beaten
25g (1oz) butter, for greasing

For the brandy sauce

25g (1oz) cornflour
400ml (14fl oz) milk
85g (3oz) caster sugar
Few drops of vanilla extract
50ml (2fl oz) brandy
100ml (3½fl oz) double cream

For the pudding

1. Combine the dried fruit, apricots, candied peel, orange juice and zest, muscovado sugar and whisky in a mixing bowl. Cover with cling film and leave in the fridge for 24 hours.

2. Once the fruit has had a chance to soak, in a large mixing bowl combine the sliced almonds, chopped walnuts, ground almonds, breadcrumbs, flour, suet, spices, cherries and eggs with your fruit mixture – make sure you include all the liquor from the soaked fruit.

3. Mix well until completely combined.

4. Cover the bowl with cling film and leave it in the fridge for another 24 hours.

5. The following day, grease a 1⅕ litre (2½lbs) pudding basin with butter (the butter helps hold the paper in place).

6. Cut a large circle of greaseproof paper and cover it with the remaining butter, then place it into the bottom of the pudding basin with the butter side up.

7. Pour your pudding mixture into the pudding basin and with a large spoon press the mix as you add it.

8. Next, take another circle of greaseproof paper and place it over the top of the pudding basin, then cover that with a sheet of tin foil.

9. Fold down the edges and secure them with string, using the lip of the basin as an anchor.

10. Next you will need a large saucepan that is big enough to sit the pudding basin in. Ideally, the pan would be the right size to hold the basin at the lip.

11. You will also need a plate that will fit inside the saucepan. The idea behind the plate is that it keeps the bottom of the basin off the bottom of the hot saucepan and helps with the even cooking of the pudding.

12. Pour enough water into the saucepan so that when you place the basin in it, it is almost covered with water. Bring the water to a boil and then reduce the heat to a simmer for 5 to 6 hours, making sure you top up the water level as you go.

13. Once the pudding is cooked, remove it from the pan and set aside to cool. You can simply pull the pudding out of the bowl using the greaseproof paper.

For the brandy sauce

1. In a small bowl, mix the cornflour with 100ml (3½fl oz) of the milk.

2. Pour the remaining milk into a saucepan, and add the sugar and the vanilla extract and bring to a boil.

3. Next, add the cornflour mixture. Bring back to a boil, whisking constantly, and remove from the heat once the sauce thickens.

4. Stir in the brandy and cream.

5. Serve warm with a slice of your pudding.

MINCE PIES

At least one mince pie is an essential part of any Christmas celebration. The name 'mince pie' actually stems from its early origins, which included mincemeat made from a blend of minced mutton and dried fruit. However, as time passed, the amount of meat was reduced and the pie evolved into a delectable dessert. Though the mince pie has its roots in England, it has become a beloved treat in Scotland as well. In fact, Walkers of Speyside, a renowned Scottish bakery famous for their shortbread, began selling mince pies across the UK in 1899.

MAKES 12 PIES; MINCEMEAT MAKES ENOUGH FOR 24 PIES

For the pastry

200g (7oz) plain flour
50g (2oz) ground almonds
Pinch of salt
125g (4oz) butter, chilled
1 egg
50g (2oz) sugar

For the mincemeat

(You can buy good quality mince pie filling in most good grocery stores.)

170g (6oz) seedless raisins
125g (4oz) sultanas
125g (4oz) currants
50g (2oz) mixed peel
50g (2oz) dried prunes, chopped
170g (6oz) soft brown sugar
1 Braeburn or Cox apple, peeled, cored and grated
100g (3½oz) shredded suet or veggie suet
1 orange, juiced and zested
1 lemon, juiced and zested
50g (2oz) sliced almonds
½ tsp mixed spice
½ tsp ground cinnamon
Pinch of nutmeg
100ml (3½fl oz) brandy

For the pastry

1. Sieve the flour, ground almonds and salt into a bowl.

2. Dice the chilled butter and add to the flour mixture. Lightly rub in the butter to achieve a sandy texture. Do this by running your hands down the insides of the bowl and going right to the bottom; when your fingers meet, slowly lift them out of the bowl, rubbing your thumbs over your fingers as you go.

3. The secret of perfect pastry is to make sure you do not work it too much at this stage. I always try and make sure that I don't rub all the butter in completely. I like to see little flakes of butter once I have finished rubbing in.

4. Mix the egg and the sugar. Make a well in the centre of the flour and butter and add the sugar and the egg mixture.

5. Gradually incorporate them into the flour and carefully bring it together until you have a smooth paste.

6. Press into a flat round, then wrap in cling film and allow to rest in the fridge for an hour before using. The reason you press the pastry into a flat round is so that you can roll it straight from the fridge.

For the mincemeat

1. Mix all the ingredients, using only half the brandy, in a large, deep baking tray and cover and leave to stand overnight.

2. The next day, preheat the oven to 120°C (250°F). Cover the tray with foil and place in the oven for about 2 hours or until the fruit is softening and the juices are sticky to the touch.

recipe and ingredients continue on the next page

To make the pies
Butter, for greasing the tin
Milk, to brush the pastry
Icing sugar, for dusting

3. Leave the mixture to cool slightly, then mix in the rest of the brandy.

4. Sterilise clean glass jars and spoon the warm mincemeat into them.

To make the pies

1. Lightly butter your tin.

2. Thinly roll out the pastry.

3. Cut out 12 circles with a fluted pastry cutter, large enough to fill the base of the prepared tin.

4. Press gently into each hole, then fill with the mincemeat.

5. Cut out another 12 slightly smaller disks (or you could use a shaped cutter and use to cover the mincemeat).

6. Press the edges together to seal. Make a small hole in the top of each, then brush lightly with milk.

7. Place into the fridge for 30 minutes. Preheat the oven to 180°C (350°F).

8. Bake the pies for approximately 15 to 20 minutes until golden brown.

9. Let them settle for a few minutes and then decant them onto a cooling rack.

10. Dust with icing sugar.

HUMBUGS

The Scots have always had a sweet tooth. There are myriad traditional boiled sweets that I could have put in this book – I even considered making Irn-Bru humbugs, which are readily available in Scotland – but I stuck with the original humbug recipe. Once you get to understand how boiled sweets are made, you can then use those skills to experiment with others.

The word 'humbug' has a complex history. When I think of humbugs, I think of Christmas, mainly because Ebenezer Scrooge uses it as his main catchphrase in *A Christmas Carol*. However, the true meaning of the word is a person or object that behaves deceptively or dishonestly, often as a hoax or in jest. The term was first described in 1751 as student slang. The sweets came after!

Regardless of the name, these sweets are fun to make. If you have a couple of non-stick silicone mats and a thermometer to hand, it will make it much easier.

MAKES 750G (1LB 11OZ) OF SWEETS

400g (14oz) granulated sugar
300ml (10fl oz) water
300g (11oz) glucose syrup
1 tsp cream of tartar
1 tsp peppermint oil
Few drops of brown food colouring gel

1. In a saucepan, stir together the sugar, water, glucose syrup and cream of tartar. Let this stand for 30 minutes until the sugar dissolves.

2. Put the pan on a medium heat. Place the thermometer in the mixture and let it cook.

3. You will find that the sugar mix will bubble and splash up onto the sides of the pan. Take a clean pastry brush and a cup of cold water and using the wet brush clean the sides to get rid of any sugar crystals that might form.

4. Once the sugar mix reaches 150°C (300°F), remove from the heat, pour in the peppermint oil and carefully give it a stir with a spatula.

5. Take one of your silicone mats and pour half of the mixture onto it.

6. With the other half of the sugar mix, stir in a little of the brown colouring gel.

7. Mix well and pour onto the second silicone mat.

8. You are now going to work between the two mats.

9. Using the edges of the mats, fold the sugar mix into itself until it is cool enough to pick up. Be very careful at this stage, as the sugar might have molten hot spots in the middle.

10. Pick up the lumps of sugar and start to pull and fold the sugar onto itself.

11. You will find as it cools it will become harder to pull and the colour will change. It should be starting to turn a little shiny.

12. The next stage is to start building the structure of the sweetie. Roll and pull the white lump out into a long strip and cut this in half.

13. Next, do the same with the brown lump.

14. You should now have four strands of sugar – two white and two brown. Do the same again until you have eight strands, four of each.

15. Place the pieces next to each other with the white and brown strands alternating.

16. Gently press the eight strands together at one end, then start to stretch the sugar. You might have to pop the sugar into the microwave a few seconds at a time to make the mix easier to work with, but again be very careful you don't end up with hot spots.

17. Using a pair of kitchen scissors, cut the humbugs into pillow shapes, turning the sugar strand 90 degrees between each cut to obtain the classic humbug shape.

18. Allow to cool completely before storing in an airtight container.

NEIST POINT LIGHTHOUSE, WATERSTEIN

HOGMANAY

My memories of Hogmanay or the Bells, as we called it growing up, are truly special. Hogmanay in Scotland is a serious business, so much so that it is the only part of the UK that sees it as a national holiday, and it was a national holiday in Scotland long before Christmas ever was. I have family stories of my grandparents going to work as normal on Christmas Day. It was only recognised as a public holiday in 1958, but Hogmanay has been for hundreds, if not thousands, of years going as far back as the Vikings.

Growing up it was probably the only time my family had a party and for some reason my dad took charge of the food, going out all day getting cakes and shortbread and lining up sandwiches. Around 10 p.m. everyone would go and get dressed in their finest and be ready to watch a show called *Scotch and Rye*, with the wonderful Rikki Fulton.

We often spent Hogmanay with my Aunty Janet, who moved back to Scotland after many years of owning and running a ranch in the States. This was always a highlight of mine, and transported me to a completely different type of experience, full of music and games.

Each area of Scotland has its traditions and food to go along with them. The big one I remember was first-footing: someone in each household would be asked to leave the house at 11.55 p.m. to wait outside with a bottle of whisky and a lump of coal; they had to wait for the clock to strike midnight, when the door would be knocked and the person, the first-footer, came into the house, bringing good fortune for the coming year with his lump of coal and bottle of whisky. Incidentally, I was never asked to first-foot as it was good luck if the first-footer was tall, dark-haired and handsome! Being short and ginger counts you out of this tradition.

Fast-forward a few years, and I always worked Hogmanay. I enjoyed the experience of running big events and making sure people had a true taste of Scotland, but I always made sure I got home in time for some steak pie before the bells.

Cleaning the house from top to bottom is another tradition that is still followed – to begin the new year with an unclean house is considered bad luck. Houses used to be cleared throughout, including taking out the ashes from the fire in the days when coal fires were common. Clearing your debts before the stroke of midnight is another old superstition!

An incredible sight to see is the Fireball Ceremony in Stonehaven. It is a unique way to welcome in the new year and greet friends and neighbours. As midnight chimes ring out on 31 December, approximately 60 men and women parade up and down the High Street swinging fiercely flaming balls around their heads. This must be the ultimate way to start the new year.

Since 1993 Edinburgh's Hogmanay celebrations have become one of the world's most popular New Year's Eve celebrations, attracting visitors from far and wide. The festivities include a torchlight procession and fireworks display, as well as traditional music, street performers, and food and drink stalls.

Hogmanay is a time-honoured Scottish tradition that celebrates the coming of the new year. Food and drink play a significant role, with traditional dishes and whisky being shared among family and friends. As the old year ends and the new one begins, Hogmanay is a time to reflect on the past and look forward to the future.

TEAR & SHARE BREAD

This bread looks amazing and is a stunning centrepiece on any table. It is what I would call a 'little work but big impact' dish. It is perfect when you have friends and family around for Hogmanay or any special occasion.

MAKES 6 TO 8 PORTIONS

450g (1lb) strong flour
1 tsp salt
300ml (10fl oz) warm water (37°C/98°F)
1 tbsp sugar
1x 7g (¼oz) sachet dried yeast, or 25g (1oz) fresh yeast
2 red onions, sliced
50ml (2fl oz) good oil
Small bunch of rocket
Salt and pepper

NOTE
For this you will need a 25cm (10in) round tin or pan. I used a frying pan and it worked perfectly.

1. Place the flour and salt into a bowl and mix well.

2. In a different bowl, mix together the water, sugar and yeast. The sugar will give the yeast a bit of energy and give the bread a better lift.

4. Make a well in the centre of the flour and add the water. Slowly incorporate the flour and water together until you have a rough dough. Tip it out onto the work surface and begin to knead.

5. Use enough flour for kneading so you achieve a smooth dough.

6. Place the dough back in the bowl, cover with cling film and allow to prove until it has doubled in size (30 to 40 minutes).

8. Tip the dough out of the bowl and knead just for a minute or two until it is smooth.

9. Next, cut the dough into two and roll each half into a long sausage shape. Cut each length of dough into 9 equal pieces, giving you 18 in total.

11. Roll each piece of dough into a small ball.

12. Pour a little oil into the tin or pan and arrange the balls. Drizzle oil over the top of them.

13. Next, you have to prove the bread. This should be quicker this time, as the yeast has been activated. Simply put this to one side; you should not have to cover it, as the oil will protect it.

14. Meanwhile, slice the red onions and place them into a frying pan with a little oil and some salt and pepper. On a low heat, cook down the onions until they start to caramelise. Once caramelised, put to one side.

15. Preheat the oven to 200°C (400°F).

16. Once the bread has doubled in size, dust it with semolina and place it into the oven. Bake for 18 minutes.

17. Remove from the oven and top with the caramelised onions, then pop back into the oven for 3 to 4 minutes until the onions are hot.

18. Remove from the oven and the pan and finish with a drizzle of oil and some rocket.

MINI PANCAKES

WITH SMOKED SALMON AND CHIVE CREAM CHEESE

These little pancakes are perfect as canapés when you are celebrating. They can be used for loads of different toppings and can also be made well in advance and frozen. The smoked salmon in this delicacy plays a significant role in Scottish cuisine and culture, with a rich history that stretches back hundreds of years. The traditional process of smoking salmon remains largely unchanged.

MAKES 10 TO 12 PORTIONS

For the pancakes
250ml (8fl oz) milk
1 egg
15g (½oz) sugar
Pinch of salt
190g (6½oz) plain flour
25ml (1fl oz) cooking oil

For the topping
170g (6oz) cream cheese
Bunch of chives, chopped
1 lemon, juiced and zested
200g (7oz) smoked salmon
Few sprigs of dill, optional
Pinch of onion seeds
Salt and pepper

For the pancakes

1. The milk should be at room temperature, so make sure you leave it out of the fridge for half an hour before you start.

2. Add the egg, sugar and salt to the milk and whisk.

3. Sift the flour through a fine sieve into the milk mix. Whisk until smooth, making sure there are no more lumps.

4. Add the oil and stir.

5. Cover with cling film for 30 minutes at room temperature.

For the topping

1. The first task is to make the cream cheese filling: put the cream cheese into a bowl and add the chopped chives and lemon zest and juice. Season and mix well.

2. Shred the smoked salmon.

3. Put the cream cheese into a piping bag and top each of the pancakes with the mixture. Finish with the smoked salmon, some dill and a sprinkle of onion seeds.

ROASTED WINTER ROOT VEGETABLE SOUP

The simplicity of this soup is amazing, using such humble ingredients that give a huge flavour. The secret of success with this is to get loads of colour on the vegetables before adding the stock.

MAKES 4 TO 6 PORTIONS

2 parsnips, peeled, quartered and core removed
3 carrots, peeled and quartered
½ celeriac, peeled and cut into 1cm (½in) cubes
1 small turnip, peeled and cut into 1cm (½in) cubes
1 medium onion, roughly chopped
1 white of leek, roughly chopped
25g (1oz) butter
4 tsp madras curry powder
2 litres (2 quarts) vegetable or chicken stock, to cover
50ml (2fl oz) crème fraîche
½ lemon, juiced
25ml (1fl oz) cooking oil
Salt and pepper, to taste

1. Preheat your oven to 180°C (350°F).

2. Wash, peel and rewash all your vegetables.

3. Chop them into even sizes and then place them into a large roasting tray.

4. Drizzle the chopped vegetables with oil and place the tray into the oven for 20 to 25 minutes, until the vegetables get coloured and sticky.

5. In a large saucepan, melt the butter and, once foaming, add all the roasted vegetables and coat in the melted butter.

6. Add the curry powder and toast for one minute.

7. Pour in the stock – enough just to cover the vegetables – and then season.

8. Bring to a boil and turn down to a gentle simmer. Cook until tender.

9. Add half of the crème fraîche and lemon juice, then transfer to a liquidiser and blend until very smooth.

10. Adjust seasoning and serve, topping each bowl with a dollop of the remaining crème fraîche.

SHORT RIB OF BEEF & HAGGIS PIE

Having steak pie just before the Bells has been a tradition in Scotland for years. My mission every Hogmanay was to get away from the restaurant in time for the 11 p.m. sit-down at my in-laws for a full steak pie meal. When I was thinking about a dish that would be fit to celebrate Hogmanay, I thought how do we make it even more Scottish? By adding our most well-known dish, haggis, to it! Haggis is brilliant at adding a real depth of flavour. It is so tasty that anything you put it in is transformed. The surprising thing is that the haggis does not overtake this dish; in fact, most people wouldn't even know that there was haggis in this pie. I have also used short rib, a wonderful chunky and tasty cut of beef that is often overlooked.

MAKES 4 TO 6 PORTIONS

600g (1lb 5oz) beef short rib, cut into cubes
100ml (3½fl oz) beer
25g (1oz) plain flour
500g (1lb 2oz) haggis
2 onions, chopped
1 tbsp parsley, chopped
1 tbsp thyme, chopped
300ml (10fl oz) beef stock (a quality cube will work for this)
1 tbsp good oil
Salt and ground black pepper
225g (8oz) puff pastry
1 egg, beaten

1. Heat the oil in a large heavy-bottomed oven-proof pan and fry the beef, remembering not to shake the pan or to stir the meat until it has browned on that side. Browning the meat is very important, as this is when you will create lots of flavours.

2. Once the meat has browned on all sides, add the beer and then dust with the flour. Stir in until the flour has all mixed with the meat and beer, without having lumps.

3. Next, add the haggis and mix in.

4. Add the chopped onions, herbs, salt, ground black pepper and the stock, then bring to a boil.

5. Next, preheat your oven to 150°C (300°F).

6. Pop a lid on your pan and place it into the oven until the meat is tender. This should take 1 to 1½ hours.

7. Remove from the oven and increase the temperature to 190°C (375°F).

8. Transfer the filling mixture to an ovenproof dish, or dishes if serving individually.

9. Cut a piece of pastry and roll it out to fit across the top of your dish or dishes.

10. Whilst the pastry is still on the table, brush it with egg yolk and score with the handle of a teaspoon to create a nice pattern.

11. Cut the pastry into circles big enough to cover the dish or dishes.

12. Next, carefully lay the pastry over the dish and press the edges together to seal.

13. Transfer to the oven and cook until the pastry is golden and crisp. This should take about 20 to 30 minutes.

14. Serve with your choice of vegetables and potatoes.

SEARED MONKFISH WRAPPED IN CURED HAM

WITH CABBAGE AND A CLAM SAUCE

Monkfish used to terrify me when I was a young chef starting out. They have enormous heads filled with razor-sharp fangs, half of the fish's total weight is in its head (the head contains one of my favourite cuts of fish: the monk's cheeks – they are a fibrous muscle that reminds me of a lobster claw). It has only been in the last 20 years that the monkfish has become very popular and because of that it is fairly expensive. I think it is perfect for people who are apprehensive about cooking fish as, despite its looks, it is a very easy fish to cook. It's meaty and very forgiving if overcooked – it won't break up. Another real bonus is that it doesn't have any bones.

1kg (2lb 3oz) clams
1 onion, chopped
120ml (4fl oz) white wine
120ml (4fl oz) double cream
½ green cabbage, shredded
1 carrot, cut into matchsticks
500g (1lb 2oz) monkfish (boneless weight)
4 slices Parma or Serrano ham
Small bunch of chives, chopped
50g (2oz) butter
25ml (1fl oz) cooking oil
25g (1oz) butter
Salt and cracked black pepper

1. Make the clam sauce first. Rinse the clams in cold running water and drain them a few times. Sometimes clams can gather sand inside, so rinsing and draining them helps. Discard any that are open.

2. Chop the onion finely. In a saucepan, add the clams, onion and white wine, and bring to a boil. Cook the clams until they open.

3. Drain the liquid into another pan. Put this pan back on the heat until the liquid is reduced by half.

4. Meanwhile, pick the clams out of their shells – you can keep a few in for garnish, if you wish.

5. Once the liquid is reduced by half, add the double cream and bring to a boil. The sauce should start to get syrupy at this stage. Once it does, add the chopped chives, remove it from the heat and put to one side until needed.

6. Take your cabbage and shred it finely, removing any hard spines.

7. Blanch the cabbage in boiling water for 60 seconds and cool immediately in cold water. Drain and put to one side. In the meantime, cut your carrot into matchsticks.

8. The next job is to prepare the fish. Cut it into portion-size pieces. You will have to trim the fish and separate the two fillets from the centre bone; if you are not comfortable doing this, your fishmonger will be more than happy to help.

9. Next, wrap the fish in the Parma ham. This helps protect the fish and retains its moisture.

10. Preheat a non-stick pan big enough to fit the number of fish you are cooking.

11. Once the pan is medium-hot, add a tablespoon of oil – just enough to lightly cover the base of the pan.

12. When the oil is hot, add the monkfish.

13. Give each side of the fish a couple of minutes in the pan.

14. Add the butter and baste the fish in the foaming butter. Remove from the heat and allow to sit in the pan for 2 to 3 minutes.

15. The fish should now feel firm to the touch. Remove from the pan and rest.

16. Slice and serve with the cabbage and the clam sauce.

FILLET OF SOLE

WITH CRISPY POTATOES, SPINACH AND CRAB SAUCE

Lemon sole is a highly prized fish. Its delicate flavour and firm flesh make it a beautiful fish to eat. It has gone through a strange time, where it has fallen out of fashion. The other real star of this dish is the crispy potatoes – the addition of semolina really changes them into a scrumptious delight.

1 shallot, chopped
400ml (14fl oz) shellfish stock
85g (3oz) butter
85g (3oz) white crab meat
500g (1lb 2oz) baby new potatoes
25g (1oz) semolina
8 fillets lemon sole
1 lemon, zested
150ml (5fl oz) white wine
250g (9oz) spinach
Small bunch of chives, chopped
Microgreens
Cooking oil
Salt and pepper

1. The first task is to make the shellfish sauce. This is a simple reduction method. Start by adding your chopped shallot into a small saucepan, add a little oil and cook until soft without colour.

2. Once you have done that, add the shellfish stock and reduce by half until it starts to thicken.

3. Next, sieve the reduced stock into a fresh pot and put it back on the heat and bring it to a boil.

4. Lastly, when needed, whisk in 25g (1oz) of cold butter and the white crab meat. Don't boil again once the crab and butter are in.

5. On to the potatoes. Take the baby potatoes and slice them, put them into a bowl and drizzle with oil, dust with semolina, and season with salt and pepper.

6. Preheat the oven to 200°C (400°F).

7. Spread the potatoes onto a tray and put them into the oven until they are crispy on the outside and soft in the middle.

8. Meantime, rub 25g (1oz) of butter onto the bottom of a casserole dish. Season your fillets of sole with salt, pepper and some lemon zest, then roll the fillets up from the thin end to the thick end (from tail to head). Place into the dish.

9. Add the white wine and then cover the dish with a piece of parchment paper and then some tin foil.

10. Pop the dish into the oven for 15 to 20 minutes. Once cooked, drain the cooking liquor (you could reduce this and add it to your sauce, if you wish).

11. Next, in a frying pan add the remaining butter with the spinach and wilt down.

12. You are now ready to plate the dish. Form a bed of potatoes at the bottom of the plate, top that with the spinach and then place two fillets of sole on top.

13. Finish with your sauce and some chives and microgreens.

SNOWBALLS

I don't know the historical origins of this Scottish classic, but I do remember the only time we had it at home growing up was at Hogmanay. This is a delightful treat and a wee bit messy to eat. Scotland has two types of snowballs: one is filled with soft sticky mallow and covered with chocolate and coconut, and this one which is cake-based.

MAKES 4 SNOWBALLS

50g (2oz) butter
50g (2oz) caster sugar
Pinch of salt
1 egg
225g (8oz) self-raising flour
4 tbsp milk
100g (3½oz) raspberry jam
300g (11oz) icing sugar
60ml (2½fl oz) water
150g (5oz) desiccated coconut

1. In a large bowl, cream the butter and sugar together with a pinch of salt.

2. Add the egg, with a little flour, and mix well.

3. Stir in the milk and sieve the rest of the flour.

4. Mix to a stiff dough.

5. Divide the mix into 8 equal pieces and roll into balls, about 50g (2oz) each.

6. Place evenly on a baking tray, leaving a bit of space for them to expand.

7. Preheat your oven to 180°C (350°F).

8. Bake for 8 to 12 minutes, until they are light golden brown.

9. Remove from the tray and place onto a wire rack and allow to cool completely.

10. When cool, sandwich equal sized buns together with raspberry jam.

11. Put the icing sugar in a bowl, adding water a little at a time to make a runny glaze in which to dip the snowballs.

12. Pour the coconut into a large bowl.

13. Dip the snowballs in the icing glaze and allow the extra glaze to drip off – if it is too thin, add more icing sugar.

14. Next, roll them in the coconut.

15. Put them to one side to dry and continue to dip the remaining snowballs.

16. The snowballs will take a couple of hours to set.

CREAM COOKIES

This is my guilty pleasure. I always say that I don't have a sweet tooth, but I just love cream cookies. This brings back fond memories of Hogmanay. My dad would always go out to local baker's on Hogmanay, just before closing, and buy loads of cakes and other treats. Cream cookies were my favourite. To keep them true to the ones I had as a kid, I have filled them with a fresh cream substitute, as that is how I remember them.

MAKES 5 BUNS

For the bun dough

- 250ml (8fl oz) milk, lukewarm (37°C/98°F)
- 1x 7g (¼oz) sachet dried yeast, or 25g (1oz) fresh yeast
- 60g (2½oz) sugar
- 60g (2½oz) butter, melted
- 1 egg, beaten
- 570g (1lb 4oz) bread flour
- 1 tsp salt

For the bun glaze

- 50g (2oz) sugar
- 50ml (2fl oz) water

To finish

- 250ml (8fl oz) double cream or cream substitute
- 100g (3½oz) icing sugar

1. Mix the lukewarm milk, yeast, sugar, melted butter and egg together.

2. Gradually add the flour and salt.

3. Mix together until the dough is slightly sticky. If it is too dry, you will get heavy, hard buns.

4. Cover the bowl with cling film and leave to prove until the mixture has doubled in size.

5. Whilst your dough is proving, you can prepare the glaze.

6. Mix the sugar and water in a small pot. Bring the mixture to a boil and then remove it from the heat and put it to one side for later.

7. Once the dough has risen, remove it from the bowl and knock out all the air. You will need a little extra flour to stop the mix from sticking.

8. Cut the dough into equal pieces and shape it into balls. You should get 10x 85g (3oz) balls.

9. Place the balls onto a greased baking tray, making sure you leave room for expansion.

10. Loosely cover the tray with cling film and leave until they double in size.

11. Meanwhile, preheat your oven to 175°C (345°F).

12. Once the buns have risen, remove the cling film and place the tray into the oven. Bake for around 20 minutes until they are golden brown.

13. When the buns are ready, remove them from the oven and brush the tops with the glaze.

14. Place onto a wire rack.

15. Whilst you are waiting on the buns to cool, you can whip your cream. If using fresh double cream, I would add a little of your icing sugar to sweeten it.

16. Once the cream cookies have cooled, cut through the bun, almost all the way, at an angle. Fill with whipped cream, and to finish, generously dust with icing sugar.

SHORTBREAD ALMOND & APPLE BAKE

The versatility of shortbread astounds me. There is so much you can do with this buttery Scottish classic. I have a friend in the States who is a fellow *MasterChef* competitor, albeit the US version, who has a whole business devoted to shortbread called the Shortbread Society. Francis and his wife Christine's imagination and expertise with shortbread is incredible. I always look forward to seeing what he is going to do next.

MAKES 6 TO 8 PORTIONS

For the shortbread
100g (3½oz) butter, softened
50g (2oz) caster sugar
1 egg yolk
Few drops of vanilla extract
165g (5½oz) plain flour

For the almond sponge
100g (3½oz) butter, plus extra for greasing the tin
100g (3½oz) sugar
2 eggs
100g (3½oz) ground almonds
15g (½oz) plain flour

To finish
85g (3oz) bramble jam
3 Braeburn apples
50g (2oz) light-brown sugar
Pinch of cinnamon

For the shortbread

1. In a large bowl, cream the butter and sugar with a wooden spoon or an electric whisk.

2. Add the egg yolk and vanilla extract, and work them into the butter mixture.

3. Finally add the flour and bring it together to form a smooth paste.

4. Roll the mixture into a flat disk, wrap in cling film and chill for about an hour in the fridge.

For the almond sponge

1. Cream the butter and the sugar in a large bowl.

2. Gradually beat in the eggs.

3. Mix in the ground almonds and the flour.

To finish

1. Roll the shortbread so that it is big enough to cover a 20x20cm (8x8in) baking tin.

2. Next, top the shortbread with the bramble jam.

3. Top the jam with the almond sponge mix and pop into the fridge while you sort the apples.

4. Preheat the oven to 180°C (350°F).

5. Peel and quarter the apples, remove the core and slice thinly.

6. Next, fan the sliced apples on top of the almond sponge until covered.

7. Sprinkle with the brown sugar and the cinnamon.

8. Bake for 30 to 35 minutes until the apples are golden.

9. Once baked, allow it to settle in the tin before removing it and placing it onto a cooling rack.

ECCLEFECHAN TART

Ecclefechan tarts are named after the Borders town of Ecclefechan in Dumfries and Galloway. It is also known as Borders tart. This is a brilliant recipe; I love the simplicity of it, and I have always been a fan of cinnamon-flavoured things. This tart had a huge resurgence recently when one of the big supermarkets started selling them as an alternative to Christmas mince pies. This tart is not a million miles away from the very traditional Hogmanay favourite: Black bun.

MAKES 6 TO 8 PORTIONS

For the pastry
125g (4oz) butter
200g (7oz) plain flour
Pinch of salt
1 egg
50g (2oz) caster sugar

For the filling
110g (3¾oz) butter, softened
110g (3¾oz) soft light-brown sugar
2 eggs, beaten
300g (11oz) raisins
100g (3½oz) walnuts, chopped
1 lemon, zested
1 tbsp lemon juice
½ tsp ground cinnamon

For the pastry

1. Rub the butter, flour and salt together until you have a breadcrumb texture. Make sure that you can still see some small lumps of butter at the end of the rubbing-in process.

2. Crack the egg into a separate bowl, then add the sugar and lightly mix.

3. Add the egg and sugar mix to the flour and butter, then using the palm of your hand bring this mixture together to form a dough. Make sure you do not overwork the dough at this stage.

4. Next, flatten out the pastry to form a disk about 3cm (1in) thick.

5. Cling film the pastry and place it into the fridge to rest for at least one hour.

For the filling

1. Preheat the oven to 160°C (325°F). Lightly grease a 20cm (8in) tartlet case. You could use a muffin tin, if you would like individual tarts.

2. Beat the butter and sugar together until light in colour.

3. Add the beaten eggs and mix again.

4. Stir in the raisins, walnuts, lemon zest, lemon juice and cinnamon, and put to one side.

5. Roll out the pastry on a lightly floured surface until it is about 2mm to 3mm (⅛in) thick.

6. Carefully line the tart case – you can use the rolling pin to help lift the pastry into place.

7. Using a spare bit of pastry, push the rolled pastry into the flutes and edges of the tart case.

8. Spoon the filling into the tart shell until about three-quarters full.

9. Bake for 15 to 20 minutes or until the pastry is lightly golden in colour and the filling has a little wobble.

10. Leave to cool for 20 minutes and then transfer to a wire rack to cool down completely.

PORTREE, ISLE OF SKYE

GLOSSARY, CONVERSIONS & INDICES

GLOSSARY

UK	USA	UK	USA	UK	USA
Baking tray	Cookie sheet	Glacé	Candied	Rocket	Arugula
Beetroot	Beets	Golden syrup	Light corn syrup	Scone	Biscuit
Bicarbonate of soda	Baking soda	Grate	Shred	Sea salt	Kosher salt
Biscuits	Crackers/cookies	Greaseproof paper	Waxed paper	Self-raising flour	All-purpose flour with baking powder
Black treacle	Molasses	Grill	Broil	Rapeseed oil	Canola oil
Case	Pie shell	Icing sugar	Powdered sugar	Self-raising flour	Self-rising flour
Caster sugar	Superfine sugar	Jam	Preserves	Semolina	Farina
Celery stick	Celery stalk	Jug	Pitcher	Sieve	Sift
Cling film	Plastic/saran wrap	Knead	Punch down	Soft brown sugar	Light brown sugar
Coriander	Cilantro	Lard	Clarified pork fat	Spring onion	Scallion/green onion
Cornflour	Cornstarch	Large pot	Dutch oven	Strong plain flour	Unbleached white flour
Courgette	Zucchini	Liquidiser	Blender	Sultanas	Seedless black raisins
Desiccated coconut	Flaked coconut	Mince	Grind	Treacle	Molasses
Double cream	Heavy cream	Mixed spices	Allspice	Turnip	Rutabaga
Fry	Pan-fry	Neeps	Turnip	Whisk	Beat/whip
Gherkin	Pickle	Rasher	Slice of bacon	Wholemeal	Wholewheat

CONVERSION CHARTS

OVEN TEMPERATURES

°C	°F	°C	°F	°C	°F	°C	°F
90	200	140	275	180	350	220	425
110	225	150	300	190	375	230	450
130	250	160	325	200	400	240	475

DRY WEIGHTS

Metric	Imperial	Metric	Imperial	Metric	Imperial	Metric	Imperial
5g	¼oz	125g	4oz	300g	11oz	650g	1lb 7oz
15g	½oz	140g	4½oz	350g	12oz	675g	1½lb
20g	¾oz	150g	5oz	375g	13oz	700g	1lb 9oz
25g	1oz	165g	5½oz	400g	14oz	750g	1lb 11oz
40g	1½oz	170g	6oz	425g	15oz	800g	1¾lb
50g	2oz	200g	7oz	450g	1lb	850g	1lb 14oz
60g	2½oz	225g	8oz	500g	1lb 2oz	900g	2lb
85g	3oz	250g	9oz	550g	1lb 3oz	950g	2lb 2oz
100g	3½oz	275g	10oz	600g	1lb 5oz	1kg	2lb 3oz

LIQUID MEASURES

Metric	Imperial	US	Metric	Imperial	US
25ml	1fl oz		360ml	12fl oz	1½ cups
50ml	2fl oz	¼ cup	400ml	14fl oz	
85ml	3fl oz		450ml	16fl oz	1 US pint
100ml	3½fl oz		500ml	17fl oz	2 cups
120ml	4fl oz	½ cup	565ml	20fl oz	2½ cups
150ml	5fl oz		600ml	1 pint	2¾ cups
175ml	6fl oz	¾ cup	750ml	1¼ pint	3 cups
200ml	7fl oz		900ml	1½ pint	3¾ cups
250ml	8fl oz	1 cup	1 litre	1¾ pint	1 quart
300ml	10fl oz	1¼ cups			

RECIPE INDICES

GLUTEN-FREE

Some of these can be made gluten-free by swapping out ingredients for gluten-free alternatives. Use gluten-free bread, make sure your stock is gluten-free. Oats are naturally gluten-free but can contain traces.

NEW YEAR'S DAY

Smoked Salmon with Scrambled Eggs	11
Grilled Kippers with Dulse Seaweed Butter	15
Porridge	17
Chicken Tikka Masala	21
Kale Brose	25
Chocolate & Coconut Meringues	30

BURNS NIGHT

Nowt's Tail	41
Whisky & Heather Honey-Cured Sea Trout	47
Clams with Bacon & Kale	48
Steamed Halibut with Salmon Mouse	53

EASTER

Poached Salmon with a Caper Herb Sauce	64
Pan-Seared Mackerel with Potato, Fennel & Herb Salad	68
Roasted Jerusalem Artichoke with Broad Beans, Buckwheat & Tomato	71
Paisley Almond Cakes	87

SCOTTISH WEDDINGS

King Scallop with Brown Crab, Barley & Spinach	94
Pan-Seared Langoustine	97
Confit Duck Leg Salad	101
Razor Clams	107

HIGHLAND GAMES & FESTIVALS

Corned Beef Brisket Sandwich	122
Chippy Pickled Onions	127
Slow-Cooked Pork Shoulder Sandwich	135
Winkles	138
Grilled Lobster	141

THE GLORIOUS TWELFTH

Roast Mallard Confit Leg	151
Roast Partridge	155
Roast Grouse	156
Classic Roast Woodcock	158
Pan-Seared Fillet of Cod	161

HALLOWEEN

Baked Butternut Squash	172
Candy Apples	178
Cinder Toffee	181
Highland Toffee	184

ST ANDREW'S DAY

Mussel Bree	196
Grilled Langoustine	198
Grilled King Scallops	202
Chicken in the Heather	205
Spiced Ribeye Steak	213

CHRISTMAS

Parsnip & Smoked Cheddar Soup	229
Honey Roast Parsnips	234
Brussels Sprouts	236
Humbugs	246

HOGMANAY

Roasted Winter Root Vegetable Soup	256
Seared Monkfish Wrapped in Cured Ham	260

VEGETARIAN & VEGAN

Some of these can be made vegetarian by substituting the meat for meat-free products. Haggis can be swapped for vegetarian haggis, and gelatine can be swapped for a vegan alternative. Chicken and beef stock can be swapped for vegetable stock. Some of these can also be made vegan by swapping out ingredients for dairy-free alternatives. Swap milk and butter for dairy-free alternatives and use vegan mayonnaise to substitute mayonnaise that contains eggs. Please note this does not work for all the recipes in the book, only the ones marked with a (v) below.

NEW YEAR'S DAY
Porridge (v)	17
Kale Brose	25
Crispy Potato & Broad Bean Salad (v)	26
Orkney Broonie	29
Chocolate & Coconut Meringues	30

BURNS NIGHT
Haggis Croquettes	38
Haggis, Neeps & Tatties	42
Brown Bread (v)	45
Whisky & Orange Chocolate Fondant Pudding	55
Cranachan Cheesecake	59

EASTER
Roast Beetroot with Barley & Clava Brie	66
Roasted Jerusalem Artichoke with Broad Beans, Buckwheat & Tomato (v)	71
Hot Cross Buns	77
Rhubarb Custard & Crumble	81
Rhubarb Crisps	83
Simnel Cake	83
Paisley Almond Cakes	87

SCOTTISH WEDDINGS
Mini Cheese, Onion & Spinach Bridies	92
Twice-Baked Mull Cheddar Soufflé	103
Bramble Custard Tarts	113

HIGHLAND GAMES & FESTIVALS
Chippy Pickled Onions (v)	127

THE GLORIOUS TWELFTH
Date & Walnut Bread (v)	164
Raspberry Pudding (v)	167

HALLOWEEN
Baked Butternut Squash	172
Apple Frushie	175
Barley Sugar (v)	177
Candy Apples (v)	178
Cinder Toffee (v)	181
Fly Cemetery Cake	183
Highland Toffee	184
Plum, Cinnamon & Honey Tarts	187
Jam Roly Poly	189
Oatie Scones (v)	191

ST ANDREW'S DAY
Haggis Fritter	200
St Andrew's Veggie Pie	211
Mary, Queen of Scots Tartlets	215
Winter Plum, Hazelnut & Chocolate Cake	217

CHRISTMAS
Carnegie Brie & Cranberry Bites	222
Panko & Scottish Cheddar Brussels Sprouts	226
Parsnip & Smoked Cheddar Soup	229
Honey Roast Parsnips (v)	234
Christmas pudding	241
Mince Pies	243
Humbugs (v)	246

HOGMANAY
Tear & Share Bread (v)	252
Roasted Winter Root Vegetable Soup	256
Snowballs	264
Cream Cookies	267
Shortbread Almond & Apple Bake	269
Ecclefechan Tart	271

DAIRY FREE
Some of these can be made dairy-free by swapping out ingredients for dairy-free alternatives.

NEW YEAR'S DAY
Black Pudding with Kale & Baked Eggs	13
Grilled Kippers with Dulse Seaweed Butter	15
Porridge	17
Kale Brose	25
Crispy Potato & Broad Bean Salad	26
Orkney Broonie	29

BURNS NIGHT
Nowt's Tail	41
Brown Bread	45

EASTER
Poached Salmon with Dulse Seaweed Butter	64
Pan-Seared Mackerel with Potato, Fennel & Herb Salad	68
Roasted Jerusalem Artichoke with Broad Beans, Buckwheat & Tomato	71
Shoulder of Lamb Stew	73

SCOTTISH WEDDINGS
Pan-Seared Langoustine	97
Pan-Seared Skate Wing	99
Confit Duck Leg Salad	101
Razor Clams	107
Crispy Oysters	108

HIGHLAND GAMES & FESTIVALS
Chippy Pickled Onions	127
Fish Supper	128
Hot Smoked Salmon & Crab Fishcakes	131
Short Rib of Beef Pastries	136
Grilled Lobster	141

THE GLORIOUS TWELFTH
Pan-Seared Loin of Venison	145
Pot Roast Pheasant	148
Roast Mallard Confit Leg	151
Roast Partridge	155
Classic Roast Woodcock	158
Scottish Game Pie	162
Date & Walnut Bread	164
Raspberry Pudding	167

HALLOWEEN
Apple Frushie	175
Barley Sugar	177
Candy Apples	178
Cinder Toffee	181
Fly Cemetery Cake	183
Highland Toffee	184
Plum, Cinnamon & Honey Tarts	187
Jam Roly Poly	189
Oatie Scones	191

ST ANDREW'S DAY
Grilled Langoustine	198
Haggis Fritter	200
Grilled King Scallops	202
Chicken in the Heather	205
Pan-Seared Plaice	207
St Andrews Veggie Pie	211
Spiced Ribeye Steak	213
Mary, Queen of Scots Tartlets	215
Winter Plum, Hazelnut & Chocolate Cake	217

CHRISTMAS
Cranberry & Sage Sausage Rolls	224
The Best Christmas Turkey	231
Pork, Apple & Sage Stuffing	233
Honey Roast Parsnips	234
Brussels Sprouts	236
Goose-Fat Roast Potatoes	237
Turkey Wellington	238
Mince Pies	243
Humbugs	246

HOGMANAY
Tear & Share Bread	252
Short Rib of Beef & Haggis Pie	259
Fillet of Sole	263
Snowballs	264
Shortbread Almond & Apple Bake	269
Ecclefechan Tart	271

ACKNOWLEDGEMENTS

I am deeply grateful to the outstanding individuals who have lent their valuable support throughout the process of writing this book. I have had the pleasure of knowing and collaborating with most of these people for several decades.

Stewart Ferguson, my good friend who took all the stunning landscape shots in the book. I am indebted to him not only for the beautiful pictures but for also being by my side during every Munro climb I have ever done and sharing his Scotland with me.

Bob Creighton MBE have been a true friend and mentor of mine for over 20 years. His encouragement and advice has been indispensable.

Margaret Kennedy, past President of the National Tartan Day Parade Committee, New York, who has helped immensely with this book.

Bernard Corrigan, a third-generation family business owner who supplied me with exceptional fish and shellfish for this book. His strong commitment to quality is reflected on every page.

Joe McDougall, the Business Development Manager at Alliance Scotland, provided me with exquisite crockery that greatly adds to the feel of this book. Churchill China, Neville UK, and Lee Jones, the Sales Manager at Utopia Tableware, also provided valuable help.

Joe Stack, from Fresh Select Ltd, is a fantastic local butcher who provided all the meat used in this book. He has been a phenomenal source of advice throughout the process.

Craig Stevenson and Christine Milloy of Braehead Foods, another supplier and friend, provided me with all the game used in this book.

I would also like to express my gratitude to Max Johnson and his team of volunteers at the Wash House Garden.

Ryan and Paul Downey and the team at Premier Produce Glasgow.

Thanks to Susie Lowe for her stunning photography that has added immense beauty and style to this book.

My thanks also extend to Alison McBride, Campbell Brown and the rest of the team at Black & White Publishing for giving me the opportunity to share the recipes and stories behind Scotland's food and pulling together this amazing book.

Last but not least, I would like to acknowledge my wife Sharon's incredible support and unwavering dedication during the writing and photography of this book. Without her, it would have remained an unfinished idea.

ABOUT THE AUTHOR

Keep up with Gary Maclean's latest news and culinary adventures on his website www.garymacchef.com, Twitter and Instagram – @Gmacchef.

Multi-award-winning Glaswegian chef Gary Maclean has spent 35 years at the forefront of Scotland's hospitality industry, overseeing the opening and development of over 80 venues throughout the country. In recognition of his achievements, the Scottish Government appointed Gary as Scotland's National Chef, a role in which he volunteers to assist with food health, education, and the promotion of Scottish produce across the globe. A passionate advocate for food education, particularly for children, Gary has served as Executive Chef at City of Glasgow College for over 25 years.

Gary's contributions to education and the culinary world have been celebrated through numerous accolades, including induction into the Scotland Colleges Hall of Fame, fellowships with the Master Chefs of Great Britain and the International Institute of Hospitality Management India, as well as many awards. In 2016, Gary became BBC's *MasterChef: The Professionals* champion, beating 47 other professional chefs. Since his victory, he has travelled extensively to promote Scottish food and culture worldwide, and published several books, including *Kitchen Essentials: The Joy of Home Cooking*, *Gary Maclean's Scottish Kitchen* and *Great FE Teaching*. Gary owns two Edinburgh-based businesses – a sustainable seafood restaurant, Creel Caught, and a Scottish deli, Soup & Caboodle.